How to Get Mortgage Free Really F*$&ING FAST!

The Book on How to Pay Off Your Mortgage in Canada with 10 Simple Steps

Brian Hogben

How To Get Mortgage Free Really F*$%ING FAST!
The Book on How to Pay Off Your Mortgage in Canada with 10 Simple Steps
www.getmortgagefreefast.com

Copyright © 2020 Brian Hogben

ISBN: 978-1-77277-329-3

All rights reserved. No portion of this book may be reproduced mechanically, electronically, or by any other means, including photocopying, without permission of the publisher or author except in the case of brief quotations embodied in critical articles and reviews. It is illegal to copy this book, post it to a website, or distribute it by any other means without permission from the publisher or author.

Limits of Liability and Disclaimer of Warranty
The author and publisher shall not be liable for your misuse of the enclosed material. This book is strictly for informational and educational purposes only.

Warning – Disclaimer
The purpose of this book is to educate and entertain. The author and/or publisher do not guarantee that anyone following these techniques, suggestions, tips, ideas, or strategies will become successful. The author and/or publisher shall have neither liability nor responsibility to anyone with respect to any loss or damage caused, or alleged to be caused, directly or indirectly by the information contained in this book.

Publisher
10-10-10 Publishing
Markham, ON
Canada

First 10-10-10 Publishing paperback edition January 2020

Printed in Canada and the United States of America

Table of Contents

Dedication — vii
Acknowledgments — ix
Foreword — xiii

Chapter 1: Start With Why — 1

Start with why you want to be mortgage free. All major goals in life start with "why." What will being mortgage free do for you?

"Wanting something is not enough. You must hunger for it. Your motivation must be absolutely compelling in order to overcome the obstacles that will invariably come your way."
– Les Brown

Chapter 2: What Is Mortgage Free, Really? — 9

Learn what good debt actually is, and how to easily transform your bad debt into good debt. Being mortgage free does not mean having no debt on your house; it means not having any debt on your house that you are personally paying for with after tax dollars from your job.

"Through my education, I didn't just develop skills, I didn't just develop the ability to learn, but I developed confidence."
– Michelle Obama

Chapter 3: The Road Map to Your Mortgage Free House   19

If you fail to plan, you are planning to fail. Setting yourself up to be mortgage free requires you to change your state of mind, and have an honest look at your current situation.

"Give me 6 hours to chop down a tree, and I will spend the first 4 sharpening the axe."
— Abraham Lincoln

Chapter 4: Is It a Sacrifice or a Choice?   27

Before you get leveraged up, you need to get your finances right. Take the guess work out of your budget, and learn some fun hacks on how to enjoy yourself with little to no money spent.

"I think that the good and the great are only separated by the willingness to sacrifice."
— Kareem Abdul-Jabar

Chapter 5: Get Your Mortgage RIGHT, RIGHT NOW!   39

In order to get mortgage free, you may feel like you have to take 1 step backwards before you take 2 steps forwards. Get a longer amortization, decrease your payments, and start thinking of debt as a tool for wealth, and not a disease you need to eliminate. Paying less on your mortgage will help you get another one.

"It's not how much money you make but how much you keep, how hard it works for you, and how many generations you keep it for."
— Robert Kiyosaki

Chapter 6: Purchase an Investment Property!   49

You may be saying, "I don't want to be a landlord!" Well, I am sure there are a lot of things you don't want to do in a day, but you do them anyway. Learn about the awesome power of leverage, the 3 ways you win with rental properties, and the difference between purchasing a new construction development, a home to flip, and a long-term rental property. Which one is the best to buy, and why?

"Someone is sitting in the shade today because someone planted a tree a long time ago."
– Warren Buffet

Chapter 7: The Rental Tax Advantages and Cash Flow 101   59

It's not about how much money you make but how much you keep. There are multiple ways to have almost 75% of your regular household expenses become tax breaks for you, each and every year. This means tax refunds, which is more money to help pay your mortgage off quicker. Learn how to master the cash flow of your rental property so that you never have another sleepless night.

"Don't tell me what you value; show me your budget, and I'll tell you what you value."
– Joe Biden

Chapter 8: Long-Term Management of Your Rental   67

There will be bad tenants but less often than you think. Learn how to screen for good tenants, and learn the top 3 deal breakers on what never to do when you rent out a property.

"Discipline is choosing between what you want now and what you want most."
– Abraham Lincoln

Chapter 9: The Sale or Refinance of Your Rental   77

What should you do with your rental property once you have achieved enough equity to become mortgage free? Learn the reasons to refinance your rental property, and when to sell.

"The only guarantee for failure is to stop trying."
– John C. Maxwell

Chapter 10: Stick to Your Plan   87

There will be another money-making opportunity, and another investment that will catch your eye or change your plan tomorrow. How do you stay with your goal, and ensure that you keep accountable for yourself and your family?

"Discipline weighs ounces, and regret weighs a ton."
– Jim Rohn

BONUS Chapter: I DON'T QUALIFY!   95

About the Author   105
About the Book   107

I dedicate this book to my dad, Peter Hogben. You were the best dad a kid could ask for, and I am so grateful for the financial foundation of knowledge you gave me. Thank you for being the inspiration to my passion. I miss you and love you.

Acknowledgments

I would like to thank my wife, **Wendy,** and daughter, **Lyla;** you both are the light of my life, and each and every day I come home, no matter what has happened, you both put a smile on my face. I love you both so much.

My team, at Mission35 Mortgages, makes going to the office every morning an absolute joy. I would not have been able to write this book if it were not for you. **Brenda Williamson,** you are the leader of the ship, and you show up with a smile each day. I could not do it without you. **Chelsea Bedard,** you came into my life at a difficult time, and you bring so much joy to it now, each and every day; your attitude is inspiring and uplifting. **Teresa Franciosa,** your love for our business and our team makes our culture stronger every day; thank you for taking a chance on me. **Monica Dubon,** your attention to detail, and commitment to get things done, pushes me more each day. **Akad Jakubovic,** your positive attitude and energy is contagious. **Michelle Cole,** no matter what is happening in the day, you bring sunlight to each situation. **Joe Giannola, Preston Schmidt,** and **Davis Carroll,** your hard work and dedication inspire me to be a better leader each day. **Nicole Daley, Kristen Dias, Christine Hoover,** and **Merl Bistoyong,** your support and love have helped me get through many tough days, and I appreciate you so much. **Doug Girvan and Brent Kinnard,** you believed in me when sometimes I did not believe in myself; I am humbled by your friendships.

How to Get Mortgage Free Really F$%ING FAST!*

Jeff Pipe, thank you for always running at the new ideas we have had together. Since we were kids, you have been my closest friend. Thank you for all your unwavering and non-judgemental support over the years.

Thank you to **Shannon Sullivan** and **Tobias Smulders.** The 2 of you have been an inspiration in my life, and your friendships are very dear to me. Thank you for your positive vibes, joy, and knowledge that you bring to my life.

My brother, **Craig Hogben,** thank you for all the unconditional support you have provided over the years. We both lost our parents and worked together at the same time. I am eternally grateful and thankful for all you have done in my life.

Thanks to my amazing childhood friends, **Scott Gibson, Theo Koutalos, Mike Thompson, and Jeff Hibbard.** You guys have been there through the good times and bad, and you never judged for a minute. I thank you guys!

My partners I work with all the time—**Bill Brach, Mitch Bates, Scott and Lyndsey Foster, Nestor Buendia, Danielle Connelly, and Jacob Poirier**—you have grown through good times and bad, and I thank you for your loyal support, through and through.

My partnership with **Remax Escarpment** and **Remax Niagara**: Thank you to **Conrad Zurini.** You came into my life and believed in the vision when no one else did. I am grateful to have you as a mentor.

To **Aunty Lana and Uncle Ryan,** thank you for spoiling Lyla and loving her like your own. I am so grateful that we have you in our lives.

David Mawhinney and **Carlos Constantino,** you have been through all the ups and downs, and have been amazing support for me when I needed it. Thank you both for always being there,

Acknowledgments

and for your amazing, beautiful brains!

My coaches, **Brian Baldwin** and **Tony Robbins**: Tony, you have inspired and uplifted me for years, and I am eternally grateful for the tools you have given me. Brian Baldwin, I thank you for the accountability you have given me in my life, and continue to do so.

I am grateful to **Robert Kiyosaki** for publishing *Rich Dad Poor Dad*, as that was the first book I read that changed my life. Thank you for sharing your wisdom to motivate me.

The REITE Club, and REIN: These are investment networks that have created a positive learning environment and an amazing networking group for like-minded people. I am grateful to have these forums in my life, to continue to teach me and challenge my thinking in real estate.

I would like to thank *Dragons Den* and *Shark Tank*. Both these shows have grown my thinking and have given me something to watch that I actually look forward to. I have grown up watching **Robert Herjavec, Arlene Dickinson, Daymond John, Jim Treliving,** and **Mark Cuban**. I am thankful to each of you for showing me how to reach for more, and for inspiring me to know what is possible. **Lori Greiner** and **Barbara Corcoran,** with your ever-growing empires, you have shown me resilience and commitment to keep growing. Mr. Wonderful, **Kevin O'Leary,** your honesty and decisiveness is appreciated.

Thank you to **Scotiabank**. It was my first job and is still my bank. I am forever grateful to this organization that gave me my first real job as a bank teller, and continued to employ me through college and university, all while teaching me the financial system. Thank you!

Thank you to **Stephen and Kayla Macintyre, Jamie Johnny, and Cam McDowell.** You guys have been amazing students that I have watched grow, and you have turned into great friends. I am grateful to each of you guys for your trust, and I am proud of how you have all grown.

Thank you especially to **Raymond Aaron** for giving me a platform and for publishing my book. The time you have spent with me, and the knowledge you have given me, will never be forgotten.

Foreword

Does paying your bills and your mortgage stress you out? Have you taken equity out of your house and felt guilty for it, because you think you will never pay off your house? Do you give yourself anxiety about the financial future and security of your family? If so, you are not alone, and there is a way for you to live without fear!

How To Get Mortgage Free Really F$&ING FAST!* will prove to you that having a mortgage for 25 or 30 years, or worse yet, forever, DOES NOT have to be your reality. This book will show you in 10 simple and easy-to-follow steps how to use real estate investment to become mortgage free. You only have to purchase one rental property, and you will learn what exactly to look for in order to pay off your mortgage in a third of the time of the average Canadian.

If you want to achieve true financial security, learn how to do it from someone who has lived it. Brian Hogben became mortgage free on his 1.5-million-dollar home by the age of 35, and now lives a life of joy, freedom and purpose with his wife and daughter, and multiple businesses. By becoming mortgage free at the age of 35, Brian had the courage to follow his dream. Are you waiting for the right time to follow your dream, open up a new business, or start something that will be the next million-dollar idea? When you become mortgage free fast, you will have the security, financial savvy and, most important, the confidence, to start that new business. You can easily take more risk, knowing that you have your family's security taken care of.

How to Get Mortgage Free Really F$%ING FAST!*

What better way than to be mortgage free?

This book will also show you how to KEEP more of your money along the way. In Brian's 10 simple steps, you will learn how to manage tenants with ease, and how you can beat the tax man. Becoming mortgage free fast is a worthy goal and destination; however, who you will become on the journey through these 10 simple steps is someone who will not only be the envy of all your neighbors, but also someone who will have a new level of financial mastery.

If you want to be mortgage free, read this book and follow each step as if your life depended on it.

Raymond Aaron
New York Times Bestselling Author

Chapter 1

Start With Why

"The way to get started is to quit talking and begin doing."
– Walt Disney

I want to be mortgage free! Well, no shit, who doesn't? But why do you, really? Being mortgage free is by no means an easy feat. Starting with why you want to be mortgage free is what will actually get you to your goal. Without a compelling reason, you will slip into old spending habits and not make the tough decisions it requires in order to be mortgage free. I wish there was some real secret sauce and magic wand I could wave, and POOF, in 3 months you will be mortgage free! The reality is that paying off your mortgage really fast still takes a long time. However, it can be done in FAR less than they typical amortization of 30 years. In order to keep a goal on your radar, you must have a really strong "why!" I paid off my mortgage on my house in 10 years. That is about the same time a doctor takes to go through med school. Imagine the focus it takes for a doctor to keep their eye on the prize of becoming a doctor. You will need the same laser focus in order to get your mortgage paid off. Just imagine the freedom you will feel when you have no mortgage—what will you do; what will you accomplish? Will you change jobs? Will you start a new business? Will you put

How to Get Mortgage Free Really F$%ING FAST!*

your daughter in private school? I did! Having an extra $1500–$3000 each month, is a game changer for most Canadians.

We live in a world today where people are saying, "I will never get a house; it is too hard!" Bullshit, I say to that. I believe we are living in a world where, yes, it is much harder to get a house, with tough financing requirements and mortgage rules; however, you just have to get more resourceful. As I own a mortgage brokerage, I can speak from experience that there is a plan for everyone! It may not look like traditional bank financing; however, getting into a mortgage today is ALWAYS better than not getting into one.

Monica, one of my students, purchased a house in the peak of the housing craze, in early 2017. For those that remember, there was something in the water—everything was going over asking, and was in bidding wars with no conditions on financing at all. Well, 6 months later, Monica was a little down when it all started to come to light that the bubble may have burst. "Be patient young grasshopper," I would tell her. Now, just over 2 years later, her house got appraised for almost 20% more. That is 2 years after the peak of the market, and she still came out ahead. The cliché is that the best time to buy a house was yesterday, and the 2nd best time is now. Real estate is the single biggest investment that MOST Canadians will ever own in their entire life. The longer you hold onto it and pour your love into it, the more it will increase your wealth over time. Again, this is not a flip-that-house-and-make-a-quick-buck; this is a tried, tested, and true formula to become mortgage free, which I have taught for years, AND lived myself. This reinforces the best quote I ever heard in regard to real estate, from a local builder who was in his 70s, and worth hundreds of millions of dollars. He said, "I have never seen real estate as expensive as it is right now... and I have been saying that since I was a teenager."

It pains me to see people setting the bar so low for themselves by saying, "I will never get a house." REALLY! If you are saying that you will never get a house, then stop reading this book—if you never get a house, there is NO FUCKING way you will ever pay off a mortgage quickly on a house you don't have! Or worse yet, I have had many students start out by saying, "I have just come to terms with the fact that I will have a mortgage forever." That is not a hard goal to shoot for. Of course, you will be in debt for your whole life if you believe there is no other way. Keep reading, as I have had many people take our program and realize that becoming mortgage free, in less than half the time of the average Canadian, is not only possible but quite simple.

Do you know how much interest you typically pay on your mortgage? Grab your glass of wine and take a sip. The average Canadian will pay DOUBLE what their mortgage is, in interest costs. That's right— DOUBLE! Now, that was the average, which unfortunately means that there are many people that will pay significantly more than double; the reason being chronic refinancing. When you refinance your mortgage, add money to it, and re-amortize it—which means putting it over a longer period of time—you end up paying way more interest. I have been teaching people how to pay off their mortgage in half the time for years. With a plan, and some specific tactics, you can do it too.

My "why" was a lifelong goal to be mortgage free by the time I was 35 years old. My father was the inspiration for me, as he lived a modest life, worked hard at his 9 to 5 at a local steel mill in my hometown of Hamilton, and lived a modest life. My dad was able to pay off his mortgage in only 7 years—now, mind you, the house he lived in with my mom was bought in the early 70s for under $30,000. However, to put it into perspective, his income was under $10,000 per year. By paying off his mortgage,

How to Get Mortgage Free Really F$%ING FAST!*

my brother and I were able to live the life of having 2 fully present parents at all of our hockey games, basketball games, awards at school, and any other important events in our lives. My dad lived a humble life, and by spending less than what he made, and really sacrificing things like a fancy car, exotic vacations, and even going out to eat, he was able to be mortgage free VERY quickly! Since my dad passed away, almost 7 years ago at the time of this writing, I am eternally grateful for those financial values and goals that he supported me with. I purchased my first house when I was 24 years old, and achieved my goal of paying off my house just before my 35th birthday. That is where the name of my mortgage brokerage came from: Mission35. I will take you through all the steps that I took, in the later chapters. Being a father myself now, the freedom and benefits I am able to provide for my family are a blessing. I am able to earn an income teaching people about something that I love, and that my father had taught me.

Today, incomes are higher, but house prices are even higher. When my dad purchased his first house, it worked out to be 3 times his annual income. Now it can be 4 or 5 times your combined household income. In order to become mortgage free, you do not have to sacrifice everything, but you will have to make some different choices. I am mortgage free on my million-dollar plus home today, but my first house was a duplex that left a little something to be desired. The first house was great for a young single guy, and moving to my next house after that, it was a slight upgrade but not a huge one.

My "why" was rooted in family values, specifically by being able to see any and all of my daughter's major life experiences without having to say no. I wanted to never miss a ballet recital or a dance routine. I wanted to be at every soccer game and every school assembly. I never wanted to have a family and be in a position where I would have to look my daughter in the eye and say, "I am sorry but I cannot make it." If I choose not to be there, it is all up to me. I wanted to have the choice. By being mortgage free and building a business that I choose to build, I am in complete control of my time. This was a goal for me that pulled me through the sacrifices of not spending money on things I wanted to, like driving a car that was reliable and dependable, not flashy and sporty. Mind you, being mortgage free for almost 4 years now has allowed me to save up and purchase my dream car, a Mercedes AMG GT.

What is your "why?" Do you want to be mortgage free, for the peace of mind that you could leave your job and start a new business? Having no mortgage on your house will give you the peace of mind to follow your passions and your dreams! Financial security is knowing that you have NO mortgage payment at all. What would you do with that monthly payment? Would it be a new home for your parents to live in, or a vacation home in the Bahamas? With an extra $1500 to $3500 a month, depending on your mortgage, that is a substantial amount of extra cash flow.

Your "why" is what will pull you through your goal. Take some time to discuss with your family, your friends, and anyone else in order to keep you accountable. Why you want to pay off your mortgage is the first step in the process, as you will have to get out of your comfort zone if you want to pay off your mortgage fast! The average Canadian will not pay off their mortgage until they are almost 60 years old. This number is increasing rapidly as debt levels and house prices continue to rise. In order to do something that most people NEVER accomplish, you will have to do things that MOST people never do.

Write out your "why," and send it to **freeme@getmortgage freefast.com**. By you sending this over to my team, we can help keep you accountable, not to mention send you a free bonus as well! Take your time and really think about it. When I teach the Get Mortgage Free Fast course, we have everyone write out their "why," in 2 forms—one from a pleasure or positive perspective, and one from a pain or negative perspective.

Most people think about the positive outcomes; however, the reality is that looking at the pleasure does not motivate us enough, in most cases, to stay on course or even take action in the first place. By associating pain, you are more likely to achieve your goal; the reason being that our brains are hard wired to keep us in a place of comfort. By associating a MAJOR pain that would occur if you do not achieve your goal, you are more likely to win than if you just associate the positive things that will happen by achieving your goal. By attacking your "why" from both the pain and the pleasure perspective, you will multiply the chances of you achieving your goal.

I gave you my personal "why," which is from a positive place, but the "why" that pushed me even harder comes from a darker space, and it was out of anger when my father passed. As I mentioned, my dad had worked his ass off for a local steel company for over 40 years. Growing up in the 50s and 60s, you were taught to get a job at a good company, work hard, and they would take care of you by way of a pension. Well, unfortunately, as a lot of us know, that was a complete line of bullshit. My dad did everything right, as far as what people told him. He paid off his house quickly, saved some money in RRSPs, lived within his means, spent less than what he made, and retired before the age of 60. He was not a wealthy man. In his highest income earning year, he made $60,000, which was enough to give my brother and me everything we needed, but not everything we wanted. In the same year that he was diagnosed with leukemia, the company from which he was getting his pension and benefits went into receivership (which is similar to a bankruptcy), and they eliminated the survivor's pension as well as the benefits that went along with it. What that meant was that when he passed, there would be nothing left over for my mom—money, benefits, all gone. What a punch to the gut for my dad. He was lying in his death bed, knowing that what he had built up for his family and his wife would not be there after he was gone. It pains me to think how much this must have angered him at the time. This was the major pain—and still is to this day—that motivates me to ensure that no one is going to take care of my family but me. I sure as hell will not be banking on any Old Age Security or Canada Pension plan when I get older. If you are, I am glad you are reading this book, because that system is broken, my friends—it was actually designed when life expectancy was in the 60s. With people living longer lives, and more people pulling from it than putting in, I would make you a bet that it will not be around in the next 20 years. As you can see from my very detailed "why" above, taking it from a pain perspective can be much more moving than the positive one above.

An example for you might be: I will pay off my mortgage really fucking fast, because if I were to lose my job in 10 years, I would not be able to afford to keep the heat on or pay the bills, and my daughter would not be able to go to university. I would be a disappointment to my daughter, and I would never forgive myself for not having the resources for her to pursue her dreams and goals, and to live the best life possible! The more detail and emotion you can put behind it, the more effective it will be.

I realize these examples may sound harsh to some, and morbid. But the more pain you associate with not achieving your goal, anything you do in life will have more staying power. Take exercising for example. I have a 3-year-old daughter—my wife and I were a bit late out of the gate having kids. My goal is to live to 100 now, so that I can see my grandchildren! It may sound a bit crazy; however, the pain, now, of not being able to see this, is great for me. I love her so much, and to live a healthy lifestyle is not a good enough motivator for me; however, if I associate the pain of not being able to see my daughter, Lyla, have her kids, just the way that my parents were not able to see my kids, it inspires me to make much better choices in order to live for a long time!

Find out your "why," talk to your family, share with them, and this will make you accountable. The more energy you put into this first step, the more likely you will achieve your goal. Make your "why" your screen saver. Keep it top of mind so that you will constantly think about it. Wherever your focus goes, energy will flow. I have a picture of my daughter, Lyla, on my screen saver; so, every day when I am at work, I am thinking about what I am building and who I am becoming for her.

In the next chapter, you are going to find out that mortgage free is not what you think it is. You can actually be mortgage free but still have a mortgage on your house. Sound crazy? Keep on reading to see what I mean.

Chapter 2

What is Mortgage Free, Really? Changing Bad Debt into Good Debt

"When you change your thinking, you change your action. When you change your action, you change your future."
– Zig Ziglar

    I paid off my mortgage on my house, just before my 35th birthday. However, I still had debt that was owing on my house. How does that work, you might be asking? I owned several rental properties at the time, and I had my mortgage broken up into 3 parts. I had the "true" balance of my mortgage, which was approximately $300,000, that was left over from the original purchase price of $550,000. I also had another mortgage on my property, for $75,000, which was the down payment for another rental property, in addition to another mortgage for $60,000, which was the down payment and closing costs for a 3rd rental property. When I paid off my house and became mortgage free, I eliminated the $300,000 portion, as that was the portion that was not tied to investment. The other 2 mortgage loans that I had were generating income, making them tax deductible expenses.
    Being mortgage free does not mean you have no debt on your house. It simply means that the mortgage or any debt on

your house is not being paid for by you! Sounds pretty sweet, doesn't it? This is where we have to determine what is GOOD debt and what is BAD debt. Good debt is not the last-minute trip you got that was on sale, so it was a GOOD deal. GOOD debt is NOT the line of credit you have on your house either! Let's get another thing straight here; if you have no mortgage on your house, BUT you have a secured line of credit or outside debt owing, you are not mortgage free! This is actually the worst thing you can do. Mortgage debt, which is debt secured on your house, is some of the cheapest money you can borrow anywhere. If you do not have all of your debt secured on your property, you are paying too much interest! Don't fool yourself into thinking that you are in a spot where you are not. I have met many students in the past who boast they are mortgage free; however, they have a line of credit and other debts amounting to over $150,000! This is not mortgage free; this is a ton of debt that is in the wrong place, and you are paying way too much interest for it, just to say you are mortgage free! WRONG, WRONG, WRONG!

Now, what is GOOD DEBT? Good debt is tax-deductible debt. That means that you can write off the interest on the debt against your income. BAD DEBT is debt that you carry, where the interest you pay on the debt is not tax deductible. For instance, on my house, I have debt; however, it is all for investment properties. This means that ALL of the interest I pay to the banks is a tax-deductible expense against the income I generate. How amazing is that! That, my friends, is GOOD debt! Any debt that is borrowed in order to generate income, can be considered tax deductible. Think of it as a mini business loan, from yourself to yourself, for a rental property.

Mortgage free is having no BAD DEBT secured on your house. Bad debt is debt where you cannot deduct the interest you pay as an expense anywhere. The mortgage you have on your primary residence is technically bad debt, by our definition. In the US, they allow you to deduct the interest you pay on your primary residence, so don't get this confused—our Canadian government, at this time, says no way, Jose! The goal is to transfer this debt from non-tax-deductible debt, to tax deductible debt, and this is done by paying down your mortgage, then re-borrowing the same amount in money-making investments.

A popular way of achieving this goal is by way of what was called, in the old days, "The Smith Manoeuvre." This is where you would take any liquid cash that you have, by way of TFSAs (tax free savings accounts), non-registered mutual funds, etc., and put that money toward your mortgage to pay off as much as possible. THEN you would re-borrow the money again to reinvest. This in turn makes the debt that you are paying, tax deductible! To put it another way, if your mortgage is tax deductible, that means that if you are an employee somewhere, and you are making over $80,000 per year, you are most likely paying income taxes of almost 45 cents on every dollar! Now, if you had let's say $100,000 of your mortgage tax deducible, at a rate of 3.5 over a 30-year life, that would equate to approximately $4000 of interest that you would be paying over the year. Now, as a tax deduction, you would end up getting almost $1800 in a tax refund! Do I have your attention now? By having tax deductible debt on your house for your investments, whether it be paper assets, investing in a business, or real estate, it could result in a tax refund at the end of the year, depending on your circumstances! This is good news! When I teach this at seminars, many people say, "But Brian, I want to save up my investments at the same time, and have the power of compounding work for me, while I pay off my mortgage!" The reality is that it is THE SAME THING! Take Chelsea, for example, who is an amazing and very sharp student of mine. She had $100,000 in her investments. She than purchased a house for $600,000, and had a down payment of $300,000 from the sale of her other property. She at first wanted to get a mortgage for $300,000, and keep her investments in mutual funds.

After my training program, she instantly liquidated her investments and brought her mortgage down to $200,000. We then set her up with a home equity program with a major bank, re-borrowed that same $100,000 as a separate loan, and repurchased the same investments she had when she started. In both scenarios, how much money does she owe on her mortgage? That's right—$300,000—the exact same amount of debt in both scenarios. HOWEVER, in the second scenario, we broke the debt up into 2 parts. Part one is BAD debt, or non-tax-deductible debt. That is the $200,000 component. The other part, $100,000, is tax deductible. This will give her a refund at the end of the year, and she is still paying the same amount— just as she would have, had she put down $300,000 on her mortgage and left her investments alone! If you take nothing else and stop reading here, I will be a bit disappointed but happy that you at least got something out of this book.

Now, paying off your mortgage fast would be easy if you just happened to have the exact same amount of money in your investments that you did on your mortgage, but this is probably not the case. In fact, as most Canadians do, you likely have a fraction in your TFSA or other non-registered investments compared to the high price mortgage you have on your house now. House prices are higher than ever, which means that debt loads are higher than ever too.

Getting mortgage free, and eliminating bad debt, will require a shift in your mind set, and that starts now. Not only will you

What is Mortgage Free, Really?

take your investments to pay off your mortgage, and re-borrow the money to buy back your investments, you will also take any extra money you have and put it against your bad debt! In the example with Chelsea above, when she gets a tax refund, where do you think the refund should go? Should it go into her investments? NO! Should it go onto the mortgage for $100,000, which she took out in order to repurchase those investments? NOPE! The extra payments, tax refunds, birthday money... should all go toward the mortgage component that is BAD DEBT or not tax deductible. That way, it gets paid off WAY quicker than any other debt.

If you have been reading and trying to be financially prudent, as I suspect you are, as you are reading this book, you likely put money away on a monthly basis. You may even have what is called a Pre-Authorized Contribution Plan set up. This is where the bank or your employer takes a certain sum of money directly from your pay cheque each week, or each month, and puts it directly into an investment. I personally love this strategy—out of sight, out of mind! If it is gone from your bank account before you even have a chance to spend it, do you really miss it? Likely not. This strategy was extremely important to me, knowing my weaknesses; specifically, being out with friends at a bar, having a good time, and hitting the ATM machine, or buying everyone a round of shots! You see, even a party animal like me can make it happen, so that means there is hope for you too. If the money is not there to spend, then you can't spend it, willingly or not!

Now, in the example above, instead of putting that money into an investment, in order to pay off your mortgage really fast, you want to take those extra payments and put them toward your mortgage; specifically, the component that is made up of bad debt. You can then RE-BORROW the money, as Chelsea did above, and make the mortgage tax deductible. So yes, it is possible to have your cake and eat it too!! By paying off your bad debt, you are still able to re-borrow and keep your investments growing at the same time. It is a win-win scenario.

A word on leverage and RRSP (registered retirement savings plan) loans: Registered retirement savings plans are not, and I repeat, *are not* tax deductible at the time of this writing. So, if you have a significant amount of your investments or savings in an RRSP, I would not advise you to take it out or liquidate it to pay off your mortgage. For one, you will have a significant income tax burden by withdrawing these funds from your RRSP; and secondly, if you were to repurchase the RRSP, the new mortgage would still be NON-tax-deductible debt. At present, Revenue Canada has not allowed someone to deduct the interest paid on an RRSP loan as a taxable expense. Now, personally, I am not a fan of RRSPs, as even though you get the tax deduction now, it assumes that you will be making LESS money when you retire. The benefit here is that you are saving taxes at a higher rate when you are working, and then paying less taxes at a lower rate when you retire. Another benefit to the RRSP is that it can compound tax free. That means that the interest you make on it is not taxed. For example, if you have $10,000 in your RRSP, and it earns you a rate of return of 5%, you are making $500 each year, and not paying tax on that interest. Hence, the term *growing tax free*. What you will find when you get to step 7 of this program, Tax Advantages of Rental Properties, is that purchasing a rental property can also be a tax deduction against your income. In years when you have renovations or other expenses, you may show a loss on your taxes, which can be carried forward to your personal income. In our model, what most of our students find is that they will be making MORE money when they retire, as they have realized alternative streams of income through real estate that provides

What is Mortgage Free, Really?

for much more wealth than the RRSP. Not only that, but the returns you get with your real estate investment will far outweigh any tax-free compounding you will receive over the years, and that is because of one of my favourite terms in this business—*leverage*.

Let me show you an example of leverage. Simply put, leverage is when something small lifts up something big. Real estate is one of the simplest investments that allows you to utilize maximum leverage. Let's pretend for a moment that you have $100,000 in your RRSP, and you are making an average rate of 7%. I think I am being generous, but why not? I would like to prove a point. If this $100,000 were in your RRSP at the end of the year, you would have $107,000. That is an increase of $7000. Now we will assume that you had the same $100,000 in a TFSA or some other type of investment that was NON-registered, and you used it to purchase a house. You took the $100,000 for a down payment on a house that was $450,000. The $100,000 was used as follows: $90,000 for the down payment, and $10,000 for closing costs and minor renovations. The Canadian real estate market has gone up, on average, 4% over the past 25 years; but because I really want to illustrate a point, I will be conservative and only use 3% in this example. With a 3% increase in value, the house would go up by $13,500. That means that the $450,000 house would go up to $463,500 in 12 months' time. But wait; that's not all! The mortgage on this house would go down, on average, by at least $8000 per year. If you add the price increase AND the principal paid down in one year, you are getting an increase in your wealth by $21,500. Compare that with tax-free growth of $7000 in your RRSP, and you can see that you are over 3X the amount, because of my friend, *leverage*. For a downloadable, colour-friendly, and print-ready chart, comparing real estate to the stock market, email me at **freeme@getmortgagefreefast.com**, and put "Chart" in the subject line.

Now, for you nay-sayers out there, who are thinking, "Well, you're not taking into account the selling cost if you were to dump the property," OK, smarty pants, this part's for you. I am not advocating to purchase a property for 1 year and sell; my advice is for a minimum of 8 years, preferably a 10-year hold. Let's blow this example out 10 years and see how it looks with selling the property. A $450,000 house, with 3% average growth over 10 years, would be worth $604,762.00. Now we will round it to $600,000. The same mortgage would be paid down to approximately $273,479.00. Now assume that you sold that house and paid a realtor 5% plus HST and other closing costs. The realtor would cost approximately $25,000; HST on that fee would be $3250, depending on what province you are in (I have used Ontario), and another $2500 would be assumed for legal and other costs. This is a total of $30,750, which comes off of your $600,000 sale price. Now, how much are you left with? We take the sale price of $600,000, less the costs of $30,750, and less the balance of the mortgage of $273,479. You are left with $295,771—almost 3 times your initial investment of $100,000! Compare that to your $100,000 growing at 7% per year, which grows to $196,715.14. In this example, by purchasing the rental property, and after the sale, you are leaps and bounds ahead of the game, but there is one more factor to consider— tax.

Let's take this one step further. It is almost impossible to compare the tax payments later on, as there are so many variables, but for fun, let me make it easy for you. If you were to take out $20,000 a year from your RRSP for 10 years, in order to keep your taxes low, depending on your income, let's assume you are able to stay at a 25% tax bracket. This means that you would pay tax on 25% of your $196,715.14, for a total of $49,178

What is Mortgage Free, Really?

in taxes, leaving you with $147,537.14. When you sell an investment property, you will have to pay capital gains tax, where 50% of the gain (net of expenses) is taxed at your marginal tax rate. We will assume you are at the highest tax bracket of 45%. That would take another $66,548.48 off of the profit we calculated above, leaving you with $229,223! This is still 55% more than what you did with your RRSP, not to mention that you are taking your money out over 10 years—if you take it out quicker, you would likely trigger a higher tax penalty. I can run this situation hundreds of different ways—and believe me, I have—and each one comes up with the investment property on top. This is why we advocate to our students to get the next house first, before commencing or re-commencing any further RRSP contributions.

I sold a property when I was 34 years old, which I had owned for over 10 years. It was a duplex and was the first property that I had ever bought. The sale proceeds were enough for me to pay off the balance of my mortgage on my million-dollar house. I had purchased this house when I was 24 years old, and did not sell it when I purchased my next house as well. By strategically leveraging myself with 2 houses at the same time, I was able to let them grow exponentially over the next 10 years, slowly paying off the mortgage with the help of some great tenants, and having the price appreciate slowly each year as well. Through the combination of the 2, I was able to achieve my goal. We will go through the steps in more detail so that you can see exactly how this can work for you.

Now that you know about good debt, bad debt, and our best friend, leverage, let's make sure that you have the BEST bad debt you can. In the next chapter, you will learn all about how to ensure that you get the best mortgage, and how to set up your mortgage to get mortgage free, really fucking fast!

Chapter 3

The Road Map to Your Mortgage-Free House

"If you don't know where you want to go, then it doesn't matter which path you take."
– Alice in Wonderland

When you are going on any trip to an amazing place, you usually have the dreaded travel day. You wake up early in the morning and fight some traffic to get to the airport. When you are at the airport, you usually have someone pat you down—not the cute one you were hoping for—and all of your privacy is completely thrown out the window. Once you have finished that exercise, you sit and wait. You buy some over-priced coffee and snacks, and if you're like my wife, a $10 magazine, and then you wait some more. After another hour or so, you line up again, only to be cramped into a small space where you have to bother the person beside you if you have to pee! Not to mention the unwritten rules on who owns the arm rest, as there is only one. After a 3 or 4-hour flight, you then arrive at a sunny destination, where you are greeted by another line up, and where someone questions you as to why you are coming to their beautiful country. After getting through the interrogation session, you patiently wait for your bags to arrive, and you carry them to yet another mode of transportation to get to where you are going. Once you arrive, you wait in yet another line up to ensure that you are at the right destination and have actually paid for your accommodations, all the while hoping your room is ready! You then finally get to your room, where you hope like hell that they have left you a bottle of champagne on ice, like you asked, so that you can finally sit down on the balcony and watch the sun set, with a cool glass of your favorite drink, only to see your first day of a long overdue vacation come to an end. However, as the sun glides over your forehead, and the cool Caribbean breeze crosses your face, all while you hear the waves crash against the shore, the journey is all forgotten, and you are enjoying the destination. It was all worth it, and you would do it again in a heart beat.

In order to get to a vacation destination like the one above, you have to be willing to go through some pain. Getting mortgage free, fast, is the ultimate vacation destination—it is 100x the feeling described above, with better views, better cocktails, and 10-star service. As you can imagine, the travel time is also respective of the destination. In this chapter, we are going to bring on the pain. For some of you reading this, it will be a piece of cake, as you may have likely already practiced some of these principles. For some—and I have taught this many times before—this will be where you quit. The pressure is on.

The road map to being mortgage free starts with where you are right now, with your current house and debt position. In order to be mortgage free in 10 years, you will need to purchase 2 houses: one that you are living in, and will continue to live in, and one that you will own and manage as a rental property. If you are over leveraged right now, meaning that you have purchased your dream house and are just barely surviving, and are working your ass off trying to make the payments, you need to downsize now. Getting a house that you can live in, and raise your family, is a very personal choice, one that you may have already thought you made. This is the time to really take a hard look at your situation and decide what your MUST haves are. This is not to be confused with your SHOULD haves, as you never get what you should have—you only get what you must have. When you make the decision a *must*, you leave no other options, and you make it happen. When you make something a *must*, you do not have excuses; you have reasons for making it so.

My first house was truly a dilapidated duplex. I remember not being able to afford drapes or window coverings, and my dad coming over the first winter, with his staple gun, helping me put up plastic wrap—yup, just like Dexter—on the windows to help insulate the house from the freezing cold weather. This was by no means my dream house; however, I was young, in my early 20s, single, and wanted to move out of my parent's basement. By moving into a duplex, I was able to receive rental income from the top floor, and I lived on the main floor. I was living for less than what it would have cost me to rent anywhere else! I was OWNING for less than rent. I could have rented a much nicer apartment; I could have borrowed more money and got a nicer house, with no rental income. I will never forget my first BBQ, and I was the only one in attendance. I sat there looking up at the stars in the brisk November air, while my no-name burger was cooking on the BBQ that a friend of mine had given me for free, as the hood would not even open without falling off—this was all mine, and I did it! I did it! I purchased my first house, and no one was going to take it away from me. I would make it work, no matter what. The mortgage would always be paid, I would always make sure that I had tenants, and no matter what terrible renovations came my way, I would make it work. The sense of accomplishment, and the knowing that I had made the

How to Get Mortgage Free Really F$%ING FAST!*

right financial decision, far outweighed any ego boost I would have gotten from another, more expensive, cooler place. I lived in this house for 5 years before I moved out.

When I moved out, I actually KEPT the house and moved into another house. This was the house that I kept, in order to become mortgage free. This was the house that I ended up selling just before my 35th birthday, which gave me over $300,000 in order to pay off the balance on my over-million-dollar house that I live in today.

Your road map will have to go in 1 of 2 ways, and will depend on your family dynamic and your spouse. This is where a lot of my students stop, as when you are single, you have only 1 person to please— yourself. As soon as you bring in your husband or wife...well, now we have a counselling session on our hands. It is common in my seminars that only 1 spouse will attend, and likely that is you, who is reading this book! Now, you may leave it for your husband to read, and he may say, "Noooooooo, that's impossible! We will have a mortgage forever." I am by no means a marriage counselor, but I will say that I am glad that I made my decision when I did, when I had no one else to SELL the idea to. I know how comfortable one can get in a certain lifestyle; however, remember step 1, and that is your "why," and the PAIN you associate with NOT achieving your goal of becoming mortgage free. You must have your partner on board, or you will be fighting a different uphill battle.

If you purchased your first house well within your means, then congratulations! You are well on your way to becoming mortgage free, really fucking fast! You can move on to the next step of looking for your first investment property, and skip the rest! The next chapter is all about getting your mortgage right, so that you can leverage up and start earning some real compounding wealth, fast.

The Road Map to Your Mortgage Free House

If you are in a house right now, and you love how other people look at you and think about you because you have such a BEAUTIFUL house, but you are stressed every day, fight with your husband about money, and are missing your kid's dance recitals because you have to work to pay for this amazing lifestyle that everyone thinks you have—wake the fuck up, right now! This is your wake-up call. The reason you purchased this book and started reading it is because you wanted something different. Doing what everyone else does will get you what everyone else has, so now is the time. Really think about what you love about your house, and I know you will find, as most of my students have, that it is their ego that is in love with the house, and not the house itself. It is much more empowering for you to go from a mortgage-free position, living in a house that is generating more income for you than it is costing you, and THEN choosing to go back into debt to have your dream house, than thinking that is what you have to do, as that is what everyone else does.

If this is you, there is hope, AND there are options!

1. Can you start to get rental income from your house? Can you make part of it an in-law suite to start subsidizing your income? Getting passive income that you do not have to show up 40 hours a week for is the BEST type of income in the world. I mean, honestly, who does not want money showing up each month without having to show up for work each and every day? I know you may not want to lose the man cave, or hate the idea of having someone else living with you, but guess what? That is what it takes in order to get extraordinary results and pay off your mortgage fast. The best and easiest type of rental property to manage is actually

the one where you live and rent out. People are far less likely to take advantage of a situation when they know you are there all the time. It is also much easier to serve any notices for non-payment or noise complaints, because you are there. All the tenant nightmares you have heard about are likely from properties with an off-site landlord. The one story you heard about the serial killer, who lived below as a tenant, was actually from a movie called *Pacific Heights*—don't watch it if you are going to do this, and if you do, remember that it's a MOVIE, not real life. Once you are able to rent out part of your house, and get some additional cash flow, you will have eased the monthly burden and will be in a better space to start on your next property—the full-on investment property that you will be managing in order to eventually sell and become mortgage free.

2. If your house cannot be rented out, or if you are just too deep in debt, then you must sell your house and start with a new plan. The new plan will be starting with a "getmortgagefreefast" certified mortgage agent that can tell you how much you should be purchasing for, and what you should be looking for. This could mean a significant step back from the lifestyle you are accustomed to; however, this is truly a scenario where you take one step back and get to leap 5 steps forward. Some of my students have downsized and purchased a house with an in-law suite, or a duplex. Remember too that selling your principal residence does not generate any tax. You are able to sell it with no capital gains; this is one way of getting out a bunch of your equity. We have had students sell the big house and have enough money left over to actually purchase 2 houses—one to live in and another one to rent out. Other students have moved

down the highway 45 minutes, where they can get the same quality and size of house for significantly less cost. Location is another very effective way of finding your ideal mortgage situation. If you have 2–3 kids, 1 dog, 2 cats, and a hamster, you may need all that space. However, you will sacrifice some time with your commute. Downsizing or commuting is the price it will take in order to get you mortgage free fast. This will allow you the future borrowing power in order to become mortgage free.

Now, I want to talk to your little voice right now. You know the one; the one that is in your head right now, saying, "What the hell is the point! What is the point of being mortgage free in a house I don't like, or where I live with other tenants, or where I have to commute 1 hour each way to get to work!" Well, listen here, little voice; just imagine that your wife doesn't have to work now that the house is paid off, and one of you has to go to work every day. Just imagine that you don't have to work the extra overtime anymore because the house is paid for, and you NEVER miss a soccer game, school play, or hockey tournament that your daughter is playing in, EVER again! You will never have to hear your kids say to you, "I wish you did not have to work so much." You will never be worried about your boss saying, "Well, it looks like your position is no longer required here anymore." Just imagine not living in any type of financial fear anymore. The flip side of that is what is actually possible! Being mortgage free, for me, gave me the courage to launch a business. I own a mortgage brokerage, Mission35 Mortgages, where we are committed to helping people achieve financial security. The name came from me doing exactly what I teach, by the time I was 35 years old. I would have never had the courage to do this had I not paid off my mortgage.

Remember your "why," from step 1; if you are not pulling yourself into the goal, you may have to paint more pain onto your goal. It is a fact that you will do more to avoid pain in your life than you will to reach pleasure.

Remember your "why," and remember the pain that is associated with living a life where you wake up every day knowing that you can achieve more. By getting mortgage free, really fucking fast, you WILL have the courage and financial security to follow your dreams.

Getting a wake-up call is usually the hardest part for anyone, but the good news is that in a couple chapters, we will be getting very tactical in how to ensure that you have your mortgage set up right. Who would have thought that the secret to getting mortgage free is by getting more debt! Before you leverage up though, we need to ensure that you are managing your money right. More debt can complicate a problem, so before you get more, the next chapter will set your mind at ease with how to manage exactly what you have.

Chapter 4

Is It a Sacrifice or a Choice?

"You only lose what you cling to."
– Buddha

Getting mortgage free is the ultimate peace of mind you can have. It is better than going on a vacation, better than a new fancy car, and even better than a new fancy house. The feeling of not having a mortgage payment every month is the most financially freeing feeling you can have. Now, what are you going to sacrifice in order to have this feeling? The challenge lies in that you are facing a long-term goal, while most other things are short-term, instant gratification, endorphin-releasing goals.

I remember purchasing my first sports car; it was a Nissan 350Z Roadster. I still had a mortgage, but growing up the way I did, I always wanted to have a fancy car. It was $30,000, and I thought it was the coolest thing ever, and I also thought that I was the coolest thing ever—for about a month. I would drive it everywhere, and I would think, "Oh yeah, baby, I am the man." After about a month's time, that feeling really started to fade, and I realized that the car didn't mean shit. It was a nice reality check to show me that the car would feel and be much better when I was mortgage free, and not worried about making all the payments I would have to make each month. I can absolutely validate this statement now, as I just purchased my dream car, a Mercedes AMG GTC Roadster. It is 550hp of badass, road screaming fun, and I can honestly say that I never felt this way when I had my Nissan. There is a bit of a difference in car—about $120,000 for one—however, the feeling in knowing that I earned it, and that I am not putting any other more important goals in front of it, like my daughter's education or my family's health and security, make the ride so much smoother. With that being done, the beauty of these types of things means so much more! The gratitude for having the car is much longer lasting than the instant gratification of getting it, when you know you should not have it yet, or worse, when you know you have not earned it yet.

Sacrifice is an ugly word, especially in the age we live in today. It means that we have to go without something, and if you are reading this book, I bet you work your ass off; you work really hard to have the things you have and do the things you do. So, no one is going to tell you that you should put off getting something, right? Wrong. I remember my dad's advice, back when I used to leave Auto Traders on the kitchen table because I wanted them to replace that dying 1986 Chevy Cavalier that I had to drive around to my friend's house and to work. He said, "You are the only one that cares what you drive; no one else does, including your friends." What a true statement, and it really goes not only for your car but your house, your clothes, your vacations—anything you do, really! No one cares about the shit you have! Everyone is so much more concerned with themselves than what you have going on.

Let's start right now to use the word *choose* instead of *sacrifice*. I chose to drive a reasonable car for a number of years; I did not sacrifice anything. By choosing the things we have in

Is It a Sacrifice or a Choice?

our lives, we can actually empower ourselves in the life that we lead, instead of being a victim to it or just waiting for tomorrow. Live today by choosing what you are going to have today—choose your car, your house, your vacation, your holiday, your hobby—whatever it may be!

We talked about the car being a major sacrifice or choice, but the biggest one of all is the actual house you live in. You may have just purchased your first house a month ago, or you may be 10 years into a 30-year mortgage. In order to be mortgage free, one of the biggest choices you have to make is the house you live in. I have had many students, after our one-day seminar, put their house on the market for sale. The reason being is that they know deep down inside that they are not happy, because they are working so hard just to have a big house that no one truly cares about except for them. By choosing a modestly sized house in a safe neighborhood, you can greatly reduce your time frame for becoming mortgage free.

Budget is a nasty word, and like most of our students, they do not want to stick to one. "It's too much work," is the complaint I hear most. The reason it's too much work is usually because you are working too hard on the wrong things in your life, or like most people, you do not want to be held accountable to your finances. By having a budget, you actually have to say no to yourself, and face reality. There are many different types of budgets—cash budgets, the "jars" method, etc.—but here is the one that we teach in our coaching program, which has worked personally for me.

You must break all your expenses into 5–6 categories, depending on your personal situation. If you have bad debt outstanding, then you will include a debt repayment account. The other ones are Necessities, Fun, Long-Term Savings for Spending, Investing, and Gifts. The way this budget works is that every single piece of income will be divided into these accounts, and I mean everything! From birthday money, to casino winnings, to your regular paycheque—it all flows through this system. No excuses. When you get used to doing the FIA budget (Fuck It ALL budget), as we call it, you will have all of your financial needs met. Here is how it works. Email us at info@getmortgagefreefast to get a copy of the budget.

Necessities – 50% of your net income. This is where people often quit, right at the start. You must take a good hard look at your situation, and if more than 50% of your NET income is going toward necessities, you will have to make some changes. This category accounts for your mortgage payment, heat, hydro, house insurance, groceries, NOT EATING OUT, internet bill, NOT CABLE, car payment, fuel, and car insurance. This category is comprised of things you need to survive. Now the challenge you face is to know what a NEED is and what a WANT is. If you are a realtor, and you have a $1000 car payment for your BMW, is that a NEED or a WANT? I would wager that some of my realtor friends will say that they "NEED" to have that in order to look successful. I call bullshit, as I have seen many realtors get by with half the car payment, making twice as much money. The same story goes for your mortgage payment. You may need to downsize. In order to accomplish your goal, you must have your spending on necessities in line.

FUN Money – 10% of your net income. This is money that you MUST spend every month. I want you to go out and blow this money; you are not allowed to save it at all. Every time you receive money in any shape or form, you take 10% of it, put it in a separate account or cash it out in your pocket, and the rule is that it must be spent in 30 days. Now, for some of you, you might be saying, "No problem! I will have that spent in an hour." Fun money is your coffee money, eating out, going to a bar, or

Is It a Sacrifice or a Choice?

impulse shopping. The reason you are not allowed to save it is that you must continue to exercise your fun muscle (the one in your brain). If you are saving ALL of your money, all the time, you will become resentful to yourself at some time or another, and that will cause you to blow your budget up. You will quit, feel entitled, and give up on your goals and yourself. Sounds harsh, I know, but it's because I have lived it myself. When I graduated university, I used to put every penny of my money toward my student debt, for months. Eventually, I would get so bored and pissed off that I would completely blow a paycheque on stupid shit, and get even deeper into debt because of the entitlement I was building. *Spend your fun money!*

Long-Term Savings for Spending – 15% of your net income. This category is for your planned vacations— notice how I said PLANNED? This is also for the new car you eventually need to purchase, and for the renovation you want to do on your house. This category is used for whatever you are planning on doing that will be a major expense in the next 1–2 years. This account allows you to STOP using credit for the big expenses when they come up. In addition, it forces you to stay within your means. You do not upgrade your room when you get to the Dominican, just because you had a few too many brown pops on the plane. You plan and spend what you have.

Gifts – 5% of your net income. Gifts were a major drain on my budget for years! I never accounted for them but always overspent on them, mostly because I was a last-minute type of guy, and thought that overspending meant I cared more. How wrong I was. My countless ex-girlfriends would attest to this. Tell me if this rings a bell for you: You waited to get that special someone the perfect gift, and it is Christmas Eve, so you go online and get a ridiculous gift card for her favorite spa (I actually did this for $500 once), all because you left it to the last minute.

With the Gifts account, you must be accountable to how much is in the account, and if you don't have enough in the account, make a gift! That's right; make one—write a letter or a personal note—I guarantee it will be worth so much more than what you think. To this day, the favorite birthday gift I get each year is from my brother. He takes such time crafting such a thoughtful personal card, with personal pics on it that without fail make me cry like a baby each year. This is by far the most priceless gift I get. Thank you, Bro!

Investing and Debt Repayment – 20% of your net income. When we taught this in the past, we used to separate them into 2 different categories; however, we now look at putting them both together. The reason being is that the goal is to pay off BAD debt, NON-tax-deductible debt, first. By having all your debt eliminated, and making extra payments on your house, you will then be able to re-borrow the money on your home, and put it into different investments, all while having it work for you as a tax advantage. This is not to say that you should not be investing at the same time you are paying off debt. I want to be clear that you must be borrowing to invest in order to take advantage of the healthy leverage you are giving yourself from your home. If you have no other credit cards, and just a mortgage, good for you! This would mean you are putting 20% of your income down as extra payments on your principal residence. Once you have paid down more than 80% of the value of the house, you are able to continually re-borrow that money in order to invest. Our "getmortgagefreefast" coaching program shows you how to set this up easily. This allows you to rapidly improve both sides of your balance sheet—paying off debt AND growing your assets. For a free, downloadable, printer-friendly copy of our budget sheet, email us at **freeme@getmortgagefreefast.com,** and put "Budget" in the subject line.

Is It a Sacrifice or a Choice?

Donations – 0% of your net income. Now, I realize some of you will not agree with me on this, but hear me out. I believe that you can donate in 2 major ways: money and time. When you are on your mission of being mortgage free, I encourage you to donate some of your time; in fact, I would say that this is even MORE rewarding than donating your money. When I was on my mission, I was a big brother. It cost me nothing, and it was one of the most satisfying things I have ever done. I was able to actually see and feel the impact I was making on someone's life, as I spent a couple of hours a week with him. When you achieve your goal of paying off your mortgage, by all means donate all that you want. I am a huge fundraiser now, for inner city education programs, Easter Seals, and other amazing causes. The best way to help the most amount of people is to make a lot of money. The more you make, the more you can give; and when you are mortgage free, pursuing your dream, you can make millions of dollars and donate it all. In the meantime, find something close to your heart, and schedule some time every week, but put every penny you have toward you, until you are financially secure.

The budget will not be perfect at first. The first thing you should do is take a look at the last 30 days of your bank account history, and see what you are spending in each category. Like most of our students, you will see that the spending is most often 60–80% in the Necessities category, and 20–40% in the Fun category. Perfection should never be your goal; it is all about progress. Perfection is a stick you beat yourself with; progress is a stick you measure yourself with. By starting your budget now, you are able to start measuring your progress. Make a goal to move your necessities from 65% to 60%, and incorporate a debt repayment of 5%. Try that for 60 days, and then make small shifts so that you can measure your progress. A word of caution!

Do not set up your budgets the same as above and just try it next month—it will not work. You must see where you are in order to set where you are going. The GPS on your car does not work if it does not know the starting point, so don't try that with your finances either.

Rewards

You must have some rewards along the way. Ten years to fulfill a goal is a very long time. Jack Nicholson says, from one of my favorite movies, "All work and no play makes Jack a dull boy." Pick something that you want to do. You should have something to look forward to each year, in addition to every 5 years and 10 years. This is why, no matter what budget system you have, you must have a long-term savings for spending account. This is the reward account, and the one that you can budget for each year, for the trip, the play off tickets, the concert tickets, or whatever it may be. Similar to the car, all rewards taste, smell, and feel so much sweeter when they are paid for through savings and not through credit and more debt.

Fun Hacks for Free!

I hate to sound like an old man, but I will risk it to say that not everything that is A LOT of FUN has to cost A LOT of money. I cannot tell you how many times over the past 10 years I have gone out and test drove cars in order to get my fix. I am totally a car guy; I love to drive fast, and I love the gnarly sound of muscle cars and speed machines. In order to get my fix, at least once a year, I would go to a different exotic car dealership and test drive something that was WAY out of my price range. I made this a fun event with different friends, and it gave me such a thrill

Is It a Sacrifice or a Choice?

to be able to drive it, sit in it, and even whip around the block.

If you are a car guru like me, and want a fancy car but are committed to paying off your mortgage first, here are a couple of fun options for you:

1. Find a local race track where you live. For me, it was the Toronto Speedway, and as part of your FUN money, or your Long-Term Savings for Spending, spend it all on an exotic day. This is where they bring in different Porsches, Ferraris, and Lamborghinis, and you pay a reasonable amount of money in order to take 3 to 5 laps around a track. This might set you back a couple hundred dollars, but it's WORTH every penny! This is a great way to get up your motivation, inspiration, and adrenaline, and to make an amazing memory for yourself!

2. If you want to spend a couple more dollars, google ultimate exotics in your area, and you will be sure to find a tour operator that will take you on a tour for half a day, where you get to test drive a couple of different cars. I did this for under $500, and this can be one of your annual milestones that you save up for in your long-term savings for spending account. 3- Last but not least, check out the app, Turo; it's like an Airbnb for cars. You can rent something in your area for a day, drive it somewhere cool, and take a bunch of selfies for your insta-feed!

If you are living in a place that is not your dream house, or you chose to downsize in order to get mortgage free really fast, then make a plan with your partner on visiting and designing the ultimate dream house for yourself. Be sure to contact a local realtor wherever you visit, and look at some extravagant homes. Take notes, and begin to mentally design where you are going to live and what it is going to look like when you are mortgage free. I have done this for years with my ultimate cottage. I have been looking for years, and I will even jump off the dock and go swimming for 30 minutes at the place we are looking at. Many realtors probably don't love me right now; however, my line has always been, "If I am going to spend a million dollars or more on something, I am jumping in the damn water!" The journey is often much more fun and gratifying than the ultimate destination.

Make the process of planning a trip part of the fun! I have 3 really close friends, and we do an annual boys' trip. In your group of friends, if you are like me, you have someone that never wants to spend any money and can never afford it; and then you have someone who spends like they just won the lottery, and you have a couple of reasonable people, just like yourself. Planning trips can be a nightmare with these dynamics, and often ends in arguments. What we decided to do was cap the amount of money that the trip was going to cost, and take turns on who was going to plan the trip each year. The cap was $400 per person, so all the money went to the person that was planning the trip that year, and our planner had $1600 to plan the weekend. This had to include all the food, drinks, accommodations, and transportation for the trip. This way, there were no arguments about who paid for what, and everyone got to do it their way, once every 4 years. One of our friends would blow it all in one night on something fancy, and we were fine with it! Another friend was so frugal that he would somehow spread it out over 3 nights. The amazing thing about this is that it creates excitement, as you don't know what you are going to be doing, and you are never going over budget!

In the next chapter, we are going to get down to the basics. In order to pay off your mortgage fast, you need to ensure that

Is It a Sacrifice or a Choice?

you have the right mortgage! You will learn about how to set up your mortgage, from what interest rate to pick, and what hidden fees to watch out for.

Chapter 5

Get Your Mortgage RIGHT, RIGHT NOW!

*"If you are born poor, it's not your fault;
if you die poor, it's your fault."*
– Bill Gates

The first mortgage I got was at 6.75%! Compared to today's mortgage rates, in 2019, of 2.89%, it is surprising that I was able to accomplish paying off my mortgage as quick as I did. This was my first mortgage, but under the circumstances, I had no other option except to pay a higher rate. This was not my ideal situation, but the reason I share this is that no matter where you start, you can still get ahead, as this plan is one that works best over a 10-year time horizon. In this chapter, you will see just how to set up your mortgage in order to pay it off really fast, and if you are like me and are maybe stuck in a less than ideal mortgage, for another 1–5 years, there is still hope. It is never too late or too early to start getting your credit application ready to shine for the cheaper money lenders. If you are reading this now, and feel like you have exhausted all your options, and that there is no hope for you, do yourself a favour and skip to the bonus chapter, as you will likely tune out if you feel like you can't qualify for any more money.

How to Get Mortgage Free Really F*$%ING FAST!

In order to pay off your mortgage really fucking fast, you need to do a couple of things to ensure that you have the best rate and terms on your primary residence. The best rates and terms will be the hardest to qualify for, and will require a TON of paperwork, and you will likely feel the same discomfort getting a physical from your doctor. You will need your last 2 years income taxes, both the T1 Generals, as well as the Notice of Assessments. If you are an employee, you will also need your last 2 years T4s, paystubs, and letters of employment. If you are self-employed, get ready for some fun. Not only will you need your personal income taxes, but if you are incorporated, you will also need the business financials, in addition to your last 12 months of banking history, with corresponding invoices. That's a lot of stuff! However, working with good mortgage brokers, and getting the best borrowing, is the best option for you in order to fast forward your payment schedules. If you have bad credit or a higher interest mortgage, take the time now to do the following, ASAP! In order to pay off your mortgage fast, you want to be getting the best rates. In this day and age, you need to ensure that you have a couple of things taken care of.

1. Credit. If you have bad credit, get your shit together now nd fix it. If you have collections, pay them. If you have a cell phone that you took out in your name for a best friend, and the friend never paid it, and now you are disputing it, tough loss, but pay the damn bill. Ensuring that you have good credit will help you along, no matter if you are self-employed, employed, commission based, or whatever. Ensuring that you manage your credit is paramount in order to get your mortgage right! I have outlined the ABCs of keeping a pristine credit report:

a. The first thing being, pay any and all collections you have. Period. Get them paid; call the collection company, and get them off your credit report.

b. Make sure you have all of your debts set up on an auto payment for the minimum payment each month. It is far more important to ensure that your debts have the minimum payments made on time than it is to make bigger payments late! By ensuring that you have an automatic payment set up just for the minimum payment, you will never be late, and you will therefore keep your credit report sparkling!

c. Make sure you keep your balance at 50% of the limit of your cards; this will help your credit increase. I have seen many students where their balance is always at the limit, and they tell me that they always have it paid on time but cannot understand why their credit is so poor. The reason is that when you are at the limit, the accumulated interest on the card will push you over limit, and when you are over limit on your cards, it significantly impacts your credit score.

2. Income. If you are self-employed, stop sweating and complaining that you are not getting the best rates from the banks. In this day and age, for people that are self-employed, it is tougher than ever to get approved by banks that have the cheapest rates. A couple of things for you to consider: Most of my self-employed students, who have paid off their mortgages really fast, have been self-employed and paid higher rates on their mortgages! Guess why? IT IS CHEAPER TO PAY 1 OR 2% POINTS HIGHER IN A MORTGAGE THAN IT

IS TO PAY MORE IN TAXES TO REVENUE CANADA! If your accountant is doing a great job, or you have a "cash" component to your business, I am not advocating that you declare more money to get a better mortgage. NOT AT ALL! What you should do is this: Ensure that all of your income is deposited into a bank account. This goes for your side hustles as well—if you have any business income, put it into a bank account on a consistent basis. Even if you are a bartender and make tips as your full-time job or part-time job, put it into a bank account! One of my students, Miranda, was a superstar. She not only had a high paying full-time job but bartended on the weekends. Our team coached her to put $500 a week into her bank account, every single week, for 6 months. This ended up showing consistency in her tips, which made it easy to use as verifiable income in order to get her better mortgage financing terms.

The next biggest question my students always ask is, "Should I go fixed or variable?" This is a timeless question, and my advice is to go variable when you can. Now, this is not for everyone, as the first question you have to answer is whether any change in the market will give you anxiety; if so, then you have to take a fixed rate. It is not worth your peace of mind if you are going to lay awake at night thinking about what type of mortgage to get. If this is you, then you should be taking the fixed rate. If you do take a fixed rate, ensure that you have a lot of prepayment options available, as a fixed rate will typically carry much higher breaking penalties if you make a large prepayment, or if you sell the house.
However, if you are looking for the best solution, I would advise on variable, and here are the reasons why:

1. The penalty is the cheapest. For most variable rate mortgages, there is only a 3-month interest penalty, which is much cheaper than an Interest Rate Differential on a fixed rate. The reality is that 1 out of 3 people will break their mortgage due to a major life change, such as a loss or change of job, divorce, death in the family, etc. By having a variable rate mortgage, you can save thousands of dollars in the event of one of these scenarios.

2. You will typically save more money over the life of the mortgage than you would on a fixed rate. The variable rates will always start out lower than the fixed rates, and as such, you are compensated for taking the risk that a variable rate has, by having a lower interest rate. This lower interest rate can save you months over the life of the term.

3. The prepayment penalties are lower on a variable rate mortgage. As you accumulate bigger and bigger payments in order to prepay your primary residence, this will become increasingly more important. We want to ensure that you have ample opportunity to pay off your house with the least amount of penalties possible. Prepayments typically come in the form of 10–15% of the original mortgage amount, and are usually available anytime throughout the year. Watch out for lenders that will only allow you to make prepayments on the anniversary date, OR if they have a minimum amount that you can make as a prepayment. Some lenders will even offer a "match a payment" option, and what this does is allow you to make even more payments if you use up all of your prepayments explained above.

Amortization

Now that we have covered rates, let's look at the life of your mortgage. Now, this part is going to feel weird to some of you. I realize that in order to pay off your mortgage really fucking fast, you would want to have the lowest amortization period possible. You must eliminate that thought. My advice is to put the mortgage over the longest period of time, 30 years if possible, in order to make your monthly payments as low as possible. Now, before you pop a gasket, thinking how the heck that is going to help you, this is helpful in 2 ways.

1. You will still be making accelerated payments every month toward your principal, the 20% from your budget for debt repayment and investing. For example, if you wanted to pay off your mortgage in 15 years, and that gave you a payment of $3000 per month, and extending the life of the mortgage to 30 years gave you a $1500 per month payment, my advice is to STILL make the extra $1500 per month payment, EXCEPT you are making it as a PRE-PAYMENT and not a regularly scheduled payment. This still achieves the same goal, as you are making the additional payment directly to the principal. This immediately reduces the interest you pay, and helps you pay down the mortgage. Some banks will even let you do this online, and it is actually quite gratifying to see, if you are a money nerd like me. As soon as you make a payment, the balance instantly goes down! I have even had clients that make a game out of it: Each time a mortgage payment comes out, they will make an extra payment to round the mortgage down to the nearest $100. This could be an extra payment of as little as $10–$20; however, you would be surprised how quickly this adds up! Twenty dollars, every 2 weeks, will add up to $2600 in 5 years!

2. In order to pay off your mortgage really fast, you will have to purchase an investment property. That's right—an investment property! Now, in order to qualify for the most amount of money possible, the banks will look at what your monthly obligations are. In this case, by having a LOWER monthly payment that is your obligation, and you CHOOSING to pay more, you will be able to qualify for that extra property in order to pay off your house. That is why you are re-amortizing your house over a 30-year period.

Now that we are looking at your mortgage, and you are so focused on paying it off as fast as possible, we are going to do a 180-degree turn and ask you to pull more money out of your house!

If you are already a home owner, and have been for some time, it is likely that you have some equity. Contact us at **freeme@getmortgagefreefast.com**, and we can send you a quick desktop appraisal of your house, free of charge. (Put "Appraisal" in the subject line.) The ideal situation would be through a line of credit, or a secondary mortgage that can be kept separate for accounting purposes. As we talked about in Chapter 2, taking out debt to purchase an investment property is considered good debt, meaning it is tax deductible. Keeping this debt separate from your original mortgage debt is much cleaner for accounting purposes in order to keep the interest separate. If you are in a situation where you don't qualify for a line of credit, you can still refinance your mortgage to take out as much money as possible (don't forget to put it over 30-years again), and your accountant will be able to carve out the tax deductible interest portion. It is not impossible; it just requires a bit more work.

Should you break your mortgage to get it right, right now?

How to Get Mortgage Free Really F*$%ING FAST!

    The quick answer to this is yes, and if there are costs in order to rewrite the mortgage, remember what you are going for here. The goal is to pay off hundreds of thousands quicker, and not just to save thousands. The old way of thinking (sorry Dad) is to save as much money as you can make accelerated payments, and to make sure you get the best possible rate from the bank or lender, and never pay any fees from the bank. Now, I do believe that you should ensure that you have a competitive rate, but NOT the lowest rate. Typically, the lowest rate will not allow you to get the additional leverage line of credit you are looking for.

    If you have a penalty, even if it is $10,000, and it allows you to access MORE equity, reduce your monthly payments, and help you get the NEXT asset to grow, then it is worth it. Take the following example of one of my students. Lyndsey had a mortgage with a balance of $450,000 and a rate of 3.89% for a 5-year fixed term. She was only 2 years into her 5-year term, and because she was super keen to pay off her mortgage really fast, her amortization or life of the mortgage was at 20 years, making her payments $2693 per month. Her penalty at the time, in order to break the mortgage, was almost $8000. At first, this seemed very high; however, let's look at the alternative.

    The value of her house since she purchased it had gone up and was now worth $650,000. With a major bank, she was able to refinance and borrow up to 80% of the value of her house. Keeping her mortgage at the same amount of $450,000, and changing it to a variable rate at the time, at 3.25% over 30 years, her monthly payments reduced to $1953.05—a reduction in payment of $740 per month! Not only that, but she was able to get a line of credit secured on her house for an additional $70,000!

By reducing her mortgage payment AND getting her a line of credit, she was able to get qualified to purchase another rental property in the amount of $350,000. With real estate going up on average by 3–5% per year (over a 10-year period in Canada), if you take the lower, a 3% increase is $10,500, not to mention that by having a rental property with a tenant, the mortgage is paid down in this situation by approximately $8000 per year as well. This is a net change in wealth by over $18,500 in 1 year! So, I ask you, is a penalty of $10,000 worth it in this case? HELL, YES!

Road Blocks

Now, I know that some of you will be saying, "I just purchased my house; I have no equity, and I don't qualify for more"—my god, don't you sound whiney already! Here is the deal: Make sure that you have spoken with a mortgage broker about this, as in many of my seminars, students have said that they had trouble at the bank. A mortgage broker will have access to MANY different lenders and MANY different options, whereas the bank has but 1 option. So please see an AMAZING mortgage broker in order to help you get this done. If you are really stuck, skip ahead now to our BONUS chapter, which is all about "I don't qualify."

If you have already seen a mortgage broker, and it is still not working out for you, this is where you have to either have a hard look at your finances or possibly make some serious changes. The first option may be to downsize, which could be a tough pill to swallow. Downsizing could give you the available equity and cash flow that you need. Remember your "why," and why you are doing it. Get a coach at "getmortgagefreefast," and we can set up a personalized plan for you.

Do not focus on the short-term cost for your mortgage, or where you have to move to. In order to do something great and different, you have to think differently than everyone else. If you have to pay a penalty, do not let that prevent you from getting mortgage free, really fucking fast!

As you guessed it from my not so subtle hints, the next chapter is all about buying an investment property. You probably already know someone who has done it, or have heard some horror stories about it. Please tell your little voice inside your head to shut up, and read the next chapter. Remember, you picked up this book to pay off your mortgage really fast, so I am about to show you the ultimate money-making move.

Chapter 6

Purchase an Investment Property!

"There are 2 ways to wake up. You can wake up thinking about what you know, or you can wake up thinking and saying, 'What can I learn?'"
— Tori Amos

You knew it was coming as I have alluded to it many times earlier. You may be thinking that you don't want to be a landlord, and you don't want to deal with all the bullshit that comes with being a landlord. Well, let me bring you back to your "why." YES, YOU CAN! First of all, being a landlord is easy; it is unemotional, and the fact of the matter is that 95% of tenants are actually good! The stories that you hear about the terrible tenants are from the 5% of bad cookies. Think about it; the good tenants make for a boring story! Who wants to hear about the tenants that moved in, never caused a problem at all, and paid their rent on time every month? BORING! Well, the reality is that this happens more often than not. Everyone would rather hear about the tenants that never paid rent, moved out overnight, stole the fridge and stove, and left the basement a complete garbage heap and looking like an episode of hoarder's greatest hits! That is a true story that happened to me once. Even in those absolutely terrible situations, the actual cost to remedy is nothing in comparison to the amount of money you make through compounding, leverage, and time. If you want to do something that most people don't, like pay off your mortgage really fast, then you will have to DO something that most people do not, which is become a real estate investor.

This really works. The first house that I purchased, I held onto for 10 years. When I went to sell the house, I was able to sell it for $475,000, less my existing mortgage real estate costs, lawyer costs, and capital gains. I was left with just over $300,000 to pay my home off! Cha Ching!

I am not saying that you need to make being a landlord your lifelong career choice; however, by purchasing ONE—that's right, ONE—investment property, and holding it for a minimum of 5 years, you will be able to rapidly accelerate your goal of being mortgage free!

Think about this: On a mortgage of $400,000, with a 30-year amortization and a 5-year fixed rate of 3.5%, you would be paying down the principal of approximately $8000 per year. After 5 years, that would give you a change in your net worth, of $40,000, not to mention the appreciation of the property. If the property value was $500,000, and we use a conservative growth of 3%, that would equate to $579,637.00. Think about that! The property goes up by $79,000, and the mortgage goes down by $40,000. That is a change in your net worth, of $119,000. The longer you hold it, the better, of course. This is also assuming that you borrowed $100,000 from your existing property and just paid the interest for 5 years. Did you hear me? Can you write this down? Does this not make you jump for joy right now? I am saying that you essentially used NONE of your own money. You just used your equity in your house to help you make more money! Imagine what would happen over 10 years! A conservative estimate would be to double that number to over

Purchase an Investment Property!

$200,000. Imagine you did this today, and you could make an extra payment on your mortgage, of $200,000—would that be the ticket to being mortgage free, while making your accelerated payments and paying off your principal mortgage aggressively?

What About Flipping Homes?

In order to achieve your goal of being mortgage free, I believe it should be strategic and planned, and reduce as many variables as possible. I have seen few people make it in the game of flipping houses. I am not saying that it cannot be done, but it is a much more time and capital-intensive way to make money than buying an investment property. The biggest asset you have with a rental property is time— time for the mortgage to go down, and time for the property to go up. When you are flipping a house, you are under an enormous amount of stress, as it is likely not your primary source of income, which means you have another full-time job. The amount of time and energy required for a flip is intensive. I had done it with my wife for years, and the amount of money we made was peanuts in comparison to our buy and hold strategy. When flipping a house, you have so many variables that can work against you in a short period of time.

1. How much did you purchase it for? Did you buy it in competition and get emotional about it, and potentially overpay? If you were to overpay on a rental property, time will heal your woes here. I have seen students and even myself overpay for things; however, believe me, it does mean a damn thing after 10 years, when you have seen the price appreciation in addition to the principal being paid down.

2. Renovations – How much are you going to spend on renovations? This is a number that I have seen far too many times grossly underestimated. Even the seasoned contractor uncovers unforeseen issues when flipping a home. This is something that can absolutely kill your profit if you have not accounted for something. There is a great chance that you CANNOT plan for everything, especially when tearing out walls—you don't know what could be behind them. I recall an instance with one of our students who, against our advice, purchased a flip that was a "sure thing." Once the house was gutted, there were structural issues with the foundation that could not have been seen by a home inspection, which resulted in spending over $50,000 extra in an already tight budget. This is a rare case but one that definitely blew any chance of profit on the entire project.

3. Time – How long renovations and the whole process can take is another issue that is grossly underestimated in most cases. When I have had clients flipping houses in the past, I would traditionally double the time that they thought it would take in order to get completed. The other issue that time creates is not knowing what the market conditions will be when the house is done. If it took 6 months longer than you anticipated because of an unforeseen issue, are you in a soft market when you originally thought it was a hot market? Market conditions can change in a matter of months. If you miss the market, that could be your profit. Again, with a rental property, you are able to wait out good and bad times as you have income coming in that is helping you cover most, if not all, of the expenses associated with the house. If the market is not right for the sale, wait for another 6 months or a year to sell. The goal is to take the funds and pay off

Purchase an Investment Property!

your mortgage, so wait for the right time in order to get the most amount of money!

What About New Constructions?

I have seen many students of mine put down a deposit for a new construction townhouse or condo. This is also known as buying on speculation. When you see a new development, and the building may not be ready for 1 year, or in some cases I have seen, for over 5 years, this strategy is better than flipping; however, it is not as good as just purchasing a straight up investment property, for one reason. You are not getting the wealth accumulation of the principal being paid down until it is complete. Take the following example. One of my students purchased a new construction condo for $300,000, just outside of Toronto. The building took 4 years to complete, which was 1 year longer than anticipated. By the time it was completed, the building had gone up $75,000. That is awesome! Not bad at all for only having to give a cash deposit of $30,000.

Conversely, another one of my students purchased a resale condo, for the same price at the same time. The resale condo, at the end of 4 years, was worth $350,000 (slightly less); however, after 4 years of having a tenant in the property, the principal on the mortgage was being paid down by $8000 per year, which is the equivalent to $32,000. If you add the appreciation of $50,000, and the principal pay down of $32,000, you get $82,000, which is slightly higher than the above example of $75,000! Now wait for it, as there is more! If both of these students sold at the same time, who do you think comes out ahead by a landslide? The one who purchased the resale, for a couple of reasons:

1. Since it appreciated less, the capital gain is less. When you sell an investment property, you are required to pay capital gains tax on the difference of what you sell a property for, less what you purchased it for, less the costs. The new construction has a higher TAX burden, making it less money in your pocket!

2. Most new construction investment properties are subject to an additional tax. For new builds in Ontario, there can be as much as an additional 13% tax on top of the purchase price! That is a huge profit sucker if you sell one right away and are not eligible to get it back. New constructions do have the benefit of money down and no time invested; however, it does come at a cost, as you can see. In order to get mortgage free fast, I do not teach at my seminars how to make the MOST amount of money, but how to KEEP the most amount of money, and by looking at taxes, it has a great impact on how much you will have left to help you pay off your mortgage. In my mind, when you purchase something in the hopes of it going up in order to make money, it is called gambling. I don't recommend it, unless it is with your FUN money.

Purchasing an investment property to rent out does not take up all of your time. I think about it like a part-time job, where sometimes you have to work a bit of overtime that you don't get paid for, and sometimes you don't get called into work at all, but you actually receive a pay cheque! Do not let the fear of the unknown overwhelm you or paralyze you from action. In the previous steps, you got your mortgage right! At "getmortgagefreefast" we will make sure you have the best terms and conditions for your mortgage, and ensure that you are set up with access to equity in order to purchase your next one.

When you are looking for your investment property, remember that you are NOT living there! I have had many students make the mistake, on their first investment purchase, of paying way too much for a place because they got emotionally attached to it. This is not the reason you are purchasing the property. I don't suggest being a slumlord, where you have derelict properties that you do not take care of, as they will cause you more problems than savings in the long run. There is a happy middle ground where you provide a nice rental suite that is durable and up to date. It does not have to have marble floors and granite counter tops just because you like them. An investment property is a business decision you are making, with a clearly defined entry and exit strategy. The reason to purchase is for rental, for a minimum of 5 years up to 10 years, and then it will be sold to pay off the balance of the mortgage on your primary residence. You are not buying it for your back-up plan in case things get tough at home and your wife kicks you out of the house, or if you think you could actually live there one day if you had to. The only reason you are purchasing it is to get mortgage free, really fucking fast!

Using the equity in your home for the purchase of an investment property is the best leverage you could possibly have. In the above example where a student purchased an investment property for $500,000, and the down payment is 20% or $100,000, which can come from the equity you have in your house already, and guess what? That is GOOD DEBT!! That's right; you are adding some good debt to your house, even while you still have your original mortgage to pay off. By setting up a home equity program that will allow you to keep these 2 different debts separate for accounting purposes, you will be well on your way. You want to ensure that your rental property is paying for your GOOD debt, and not you personally out of your pocket, AND that you are still continually paying down your mortgage.

What if you have NO equity in your house? That is something I hear a lot, and maybe you do not have enough money in order to get a line of credit. If you don't have the funds for a down payment, then start asking your friends. Co-investing is VERY popular today. There is no reason why you and 4 of your friends cannot purchase a house all together. Maybe you cannot get $100,000 in order to purchase your own investment property; however, you can maybe get $25,000. Why not split that with 4 other people and get a rental property all together! This means that your payout will be less in 5–10 years when you go to sell; however, it will be WAY MORE than if you decide to do nothing and say to yourself, "Oh well, I could not make it work."

FREE BONUS – Email our team at freeme@getmortgagefreefast.com, and put "Cash flow" in the subject line, and we will send you a tool to analyze your potential investments!

"I don't qualify for a mortgage with a bank for an investment property."

I have heard this many times, and I am certain that there is always a way; you just need a plan. I am a strong advocate for borrowing even at higher interest rates in order to get into an investment property, as in the majority of the cases with our students, the higher interest rates are still marginally small in comparison to the price appreciation and principal pay down that you earn over the next 5–10 years. See more on this in our

Purchase an Investment Property!

Bonus Chapter, where we dig deep into private lending.

My overachievers! This is for all of you students out there looking for extra credit. There is nothing stopping you from purchasing 2 rental properties, or 5; or heck, even over 20, like me! The more you purchase, the faster you will achieve your goal. The power of leverage works exponentially quicker the more that you do it. If you are in a position right now, as many of my students are, where you have lived in your house for 5 years and are thinking about moving, or staying and renovating, and have accumulated $200,000 to $300,000 in equity, you may be able to easily afford 2 rental properties instead of 1. My word of caution to you: Start with one, get it up and running, and wait a minimum of 6 months from the closing date before you purchase the next one. You need to have an understanding of how to rent a property, getting your paperwork in order, and realizing the positive cash flow for a couple of months, before you pull the trigger on the 2nd one. After 6 months, you will have a steady tenant, know any immediate issues or concerns with the property, and will have the confidence and newly formed systems to start to leverage the next one.

Are you interested in beating the tax man? Of course, you are! In the next chapter, I am going to show you some very simple ways to reduce your income taxes, which is actually the number one expense that most people have in their entire life!

Chapter 7

The Rental Tax Advantages and Cash Flow 101

"The only difference between a tax man and a taxidermist is that the taxidermist leaves the skin."
– Mark Twain

When I purchased my first house, which was a duplex, I was working for a major bank, making a small entry level salary. Since my goal was to be mortgage free by 35, I knew I needed at least 1 side hustle and had to really grow my income. I decided to start a home-based business, one of those "multi-level marketing" or network marketing businesses. The company that I joined sold high-end household products, such as toothpaste, shampoo, conditioner, and toilet paper, to other people. This actually taught me more about rejection than anything else, and if I am honest, saying that I "sold" anything is a bit of a stretch. In my early 20s, network marketing was not my road to financial security, but it did give me some much-needed income tax deduction. By having a home-based business, you now qualify for some of the self-employed income tax savings such as writing off a portion of your interest on your mortgage, heat, and property taxes. Any cost that is related to you having a home-based office can be used in proportion to your expenses to run it. Our team at "getmortgagefreefast" encourages all of our students to start a home-based business if they currently do not have any form of self-employed or commission-based income. It will not only give you the much-needed income tax deductions, but you will also surround yourself with motivated people who have a goal just like you! There are hundreds if not thousands of different network marketing companies today. Find one that interests you, with LOW startup costs (another tax deduction). I have seen ones for cookware, vitamins, supplements, beauty products, and skin care—you name it. If you have a job working for someone else, find a network marketing company that you can join. You will get some immediate tax benefits that you can utilize on your monthly expenses, not to mention that you may actually find a side hustle that you love, and make a ton of money from it! Luckily for me, I was also really good with numbers, and my passion was in mortgages. I eventually switched to a commission-based mortgage agent for a major bank. I replaced my income tax deductions that I was receiving from the network marketing business, over to my new role. Commission salespeople can have the same advantage here for their home expenses as the network marketing example. Not only could I continue to write off a portion of my living expenses as a home office expense on my taxes, but now that I was able to work from home, I could do mortgage applications in my underwear.

The ultimate sweet spot! The best way to maximize tax efficiencies would be the following: Live in a duplex, and have some sort of self-employed or commission-based income. In this scenario, which I used for years, and recommend to all my students who are starting out, you are able to write down an enormous percentage of your expenses. First of all, with a duplex, you are writing down 50% of the expenses, such as

The Rental Tax Advantages and Cash Flow 101

property taxes, heat, hydro, and house insurance; not to mention interest on the mortgage! What this means is that 50% of all the expenses it takes to run the house, are eligible as an expense toward the income you generate. For simple math, if you receive rental income of $1000 per month, and your heating bill is $100, $50 of that bill would be an expense against the income. By including these expenses, you are reducing your tax bill, which allows you to keep more money in your pocket. You have to pay the heating bill regardless if someone lives with you or not, and the same goes for all your other expenses. By using these tax advantages, you are reducing your taxable income, which means more money for you to pay off your mortgage really fucking fast!

Not all duplexes are created equally. I have one very ambitious student, Nick, who decided to live in the basement apartment of his house. He had a 3-bedroom, 2-bathroom, upstairs unit, and a 1-bedroom bachelor unit in the basement. The basement unit was only 25% of the whole house, which means that he was able to use 75% of the household expenses as a tax deduction against the income. He was only paying 25% of the interest on his mortgage, as 75% was a tax deduction against his income. The expenses you can account for that we are referring to here are in direct proportion to the amount of space the "rental" portion takes up in the house. In Nick's example, the rental portion of the house was 75%, so he could use 75% of the expenses. If it was only 50% of the house, then only 50% would apply. If you have a family with a big home, and you rent out the basement, you may only be able to use 25% as an expense. Remember not to be too greedy, and have a professional accountant review your numbers. The last thing you want is Canada Revenue Agency paying you a visit, and you having to justify all the big juicy expenses you used as income tax deductions.

Second of all, with a home-based business, you have an office in your home, so that would equate for up to another 20–25% of your 50%! Of course, remember the rule where my accountant always says that the pig can get fat but the hog will get slaughtered. Utilizing both strategies can add up to almost 75% of your household expenses being written down against your income taxes! This is huge money that compounds over time. It is just as important to count the money that you keep in your pocket as the money that you make. This is the ideal situation in order to get mortgage free really fast.

As my accountant always told me about the pig, remember that you can be aggressive, but don't be stupid when it comes to claiming business expenses. If you are planting a new garden in the rental property, and happen to get a couple of cedar trees for your own place, then so be it. However, if you completely renovate your kitchen at home with stainless steel, high-end WOLF appliances, and decide to write that expense off toward your rental, you may be getting into the "slaughtered" area that my accountant was talking about. Be sure to be reasonable but creative where you can. Making sure that you keep receipts for all of the expenses related to your investment property will help you bring the taxable income down. There is how much income you declare on your rental property, and how much you are really making. It is quite possible that you would be able to bring your income into the negative when you do your taxes. If you actually lose money on your rental property, don't panic. If you do lose money on your rental one year, or even two, I am sure it will not be by much; regardless, all losses are able to be deducted against your personal income. That means that if you lost $5000 in one year because of a vacancy, or even a major renovation like a new furnace, you would be able to write that

The Rental Tax Advantages and Cash Flow 101

income off against your employment income; therefore making your income taxes less! In this example, if you made $90,000 in a year, and lost $5000 on your rental, that would be the equivalent to making $85,000, which would give you a tax refund of almost 40% on your $5000 loss, OR in real dollars, $2000! Now your $5000 loss is really only a $3000 net loss. However, the monthly or annual cash flow that you receive on your rental property is the smallest of the major benefits you are getting from owning a rental property. Keep reading to find out what I mean.

On the other hand, when you have a surplus of cash flow at the end of the year from your rental income, which is the goal, DO NOT make any extra payments to your mortgage on your rental. I repeat, do not make any extra payments to either the mortgage on your rental property OR the down payment that you may have borrowed for the rental property. That may be what you would think is a good idea, but the reality is that you want to put that money on your PRIMARY residence mortgage. Remember good debt vs bad debt? The principal residence mortgage, or mortgage on the house where you live, is NOT tax deductible. You have no tax advantages on that debt at all, so you should pay that one off FIRST with any extra cash flow you have. The interest on the rental property mortgage is being written off against the income each and every year. Therefore, the goal is to NOT pay it off as soon as possible. This is another reason why you will also take the LONGEST amortization possible on your rental property. This will help you create positive cash flow, and help you manage the expenses, as well as get you some extra money to pay off your mortgage.

Each year on your investment property, you will pay a portion of your principal. Even with an amortization of 30 years, you will still be paying down the balance. On a typical $500,000 mortgage, with a 4% interest rate and a 30-year amortization, you would pay down over $9000 per year on the mortgage. Or better yet, I should reiterate, your TENANTS will be paying that amount down. That's right; the rental income you are receiving is going to pay the mortgage payment. You may have some money left over each month, but the real bonus comes in that your principal on your rental property is being paid down by somebody else! Remember when I told you earlier to not worry too much if you have a year or 2 where expenses are higher and your cash flow is negative? This is why. This should be illegal, it's so good. In addition to the principal pay down, you are also looking at appreciation on the asset each year. On average, the real estate market in Canada has gone up by almost 4% per year over the past 50 years. If you were to take a property with a value of $500,000, and a mortgage of $400,000, the price will go up by over $20,000 per year, and the mortgage will do down by over $8000 per year. This is a change in net worth or your wealth by over $28,000 per year! You can see that the net change in your wealth, in this example, over 10 years, would be over $320,000! Now, take that money in addition to the principal pay down you have taken into consideration on your own mortgage over the past 10 years, and you can do the math. You could be mortgage free in 10 years!

Cash Flow Concerns

Always keep your cash flow separate from your regular everyday account. I know some of you will be much more detailed than I am; however, keep it separate. This is good for your own peace of mind, specifically for your accounting. By having a separate bank account, you can never "fool" yourself into how much you do or do not have each month from your rental. This is also a very clear indicator to show how much money you have left over at the end of the year. Hopefully, you are in the PLUS! If you are in the positive, then it is a good opportunity to evaluate what renovations are coming up, and if any expenses NEED to be done on the house. If so, use your cash flow that has built up, and if possible, have a budget that is what you have in your rental account. Now, if you do not have any renovations or expenses coming up, then take 50% of what is in your rental bank account, and make a PRE-PAYMENT on your PRINCIPAL residence—NOT the RENTAL! Remember again that the interest you pay on your rental is tax deductible, and on your principal residence, it is not. You always want to pay off the bad debt first, and keep the good debt.

Now, if you have an expense that is OVER and ABOVE what is available in your rental bank account, you will need to put money in the account from your own personal reserves. Do not dip into your savings or RRSP for this. My advice is to have a line of credit or a credit facility that you can use to inject money into your bank account. Why more debt, you ask? Because it is good debt! If you have a line of credit available for $10,000, keep it as your rental property line of credit; and if you have to get a new furnace that you did not foresee, for $4000, you can put it on your line of credit. Now ensure that you are making just the interest payments on this debt, as the debt on this line of credit is tax deductible! You guessed it; as it is attributed to your rental property, which is a business, you are able to deduct the expense for the interest you are paying for it. This keeps your savings intact, and in addition keeps your business running as a business. The additional debt taken out for any expenses will be paid off on the sale of the property. I know you feel this terrible urge to pay it off right away, but don't do it! Take any extra money and continue to put it toward your primary residence. This book is about how to pay off your mortgage really fucking fast, not about how to pay off your line of credit really fucking fast. You must resist the temptation to pay this off as it will form a stronger mental will, and start to train your brain about good debt and bad debt. Even today, I still have moments where I want to pay off a line of credit that I have taken out to purchase a property or to make a mortgage investment, but I remind myself that it is GOOD debt and does not have to be paid off.

So, the numbers make sense; however, you never really wanted to become a landlord, because all tenants are terrible and out to get you, right? WRONG! In the next chapter, you will learn all about managing tenant relationships, and some simple key steps to take to ensure that you always start off on the right foot. By the end of the next chapter, you will be applying for the award of Landlord of the Year!

Chapter 8

Long-Term Management of Your Rental

"Beware of little expenses. A small leak will sink a great ship."
— Benjamin Franklin

I am sure you have heard the stories about the tenant from hell: He never paid; he skipped out on the rent and stole the washer; she threw wild parties, and all the neighbors hated them; she stole the copper from the house; he started a meth lab. I have had all of these happen to me, except the meth lab. My personal favourite was when a tenant called me and said there was a sewer backup in the basement apartment of a triplex I had. I had never witnessed one of these before, and I thought there was no way it could be as bad as it sounds. Well, I was very, very wrong. It was much worse than anything I could have imagined. I got to the house, and the tenant was waiting outside. I thought to myself that this cannot be a good sign. When we entered her unit, the smell hit me like a punch in the gut. I immediately called Roto-Rooter to come and help, but they notified me that it was a busy night for them, and it would be a couple of hours before they would be there. The tenant was so upset about all her belongings getting ruined that I started trudging through the literal shit in order to get some of her stuff out of the apartment before it was too late. I spent 2 hours doing this before any other help arrived, and I then immediately proceeded to go home and burn my shoes and all the other clothes I was wearing. This was a great learning experience, and from owning over 50 different houses, with multiple different tenants and issues, I now fully understand that when you own a property, you do not have to go there yourself! You can pay for the professionals to go and make sure that everything works out okay.

The reality is that all of those problems come and go, and there are ways to deal with them quickly and efficiently. The other reality is that these issues are not the norm; they are good stories that everyone likes to share at a party.

Getting good tenants in the first place can avoid a lot of the issues and horror stories you hear from people. Most people who rent are good people who pay their bills and respect the property. This has been the case for myself and our students almost 95% of the time. When you are screening your tenants, be sure to ask for a couple of things—not just the most recent landlord's info, but the 2 most recent landlords'. A current landlord that has a tenant from hell may be more likely to lie during a reference check, just to be rid of the problem, whereas a previous landlord will not have any issue to lie about in regard to what the tenant was like, good or bad. This check works well in conjunction with a credit check. A credit check will also show you the 2 most previous addresses, which you can match up with the landlord reference checks. Speaking of credit checks, do not be afraid of bad credit. Bad credit does not equal a bad tenant. It is proven that the majority of Canadians will let all other expenses lapse—credit cards, cell phones, even hydro or heat—before they will miss their shelter payments. One of your tenants having a bad credit score should probe you to ask more questions, but not necessitate an automatic no-deal. However,

Long-Term Management of Your Rental

you do want to look for collections from property management companies on the credit report. If you see one, then it is cause to run and to turn them down as a perspective tenant. A collection from a property management company means that they either missed rent payments, left the unit with damages, or have some sort of unresolved issue with a property where they lived.

Here are a couple of tricks to find the best tenants, which we teach all of our students:

1. Give the rental application out at an open house, when they are viewing the property. Be sure to collect the name and address of where they are living now. Contact them the next day, and say that you are in the area to pick up the application form. This way you can actually get a glimpse into where and how they live right now.

2. When you have a prospective tenant, have 3 sets of questions in an email: Why are you moving from your current residence? Who will be living in the new property? How long do you plan on staying? When you have received the email, and you call to do the verification, ask the same 3 questions again, and advise that you lost the email. If they are significantly different answers than the ones that were on the email, then there is an issue with the integrity of what they are telling you. This is a great way for you to test the validity of what people are telling you. When people tell you the truth, there is no reason for the story to change.

3. Be aware of people that need to move in right away. Most tenants that are responsible will not only give their current

landlord 60 days' notice, but they will also be planning ahead as to where they want to move and when. Someone who needs to move in this weekend could be facing an eviction from somewhere else. Be aware of these types of tenants.

4. I said it before, and I will say it again! No first and last month's rent, no keys. This is an absolute deal breaker at all times. I have had it where a tenant had a moving truck in the driveway and wanted to pay me on Monday, and I said, "Unfortunately, I need you to go to the ATM right now to pay me the balance in order to get the keys today." If you start out by being a credit card on day one, you have set the tone of your entire relationship. Having first and last month's rent paid in full, via cash or certified cheque, is a non-negotiable. If there are going to be issues with a tenant, you will likely be finding out in the first 30–60 days, and by having last month's rent in place, you will have a buffer zone in your cash flow to keep you afloat during the eviction process.

Now, if you are purchasing a rental for the sole purpose of being mortgage free, my advice is to manage it yourself. When I say "manage" it yourself, I am not saying "do it" all yourself. The difference is that you are meeting with the contractors and the tenant, and are ensuring that you have priced out the job with at least 2 different people to ensure that you are getting the job done right. You need to be vigilant in managing your expenses and keeping a close eye on your investment. Property managers are great, and I have one today, but not all of them are created equal. I would not know what the true cost of things are had I not managed my own properties for years. It is imperative that you know how much things cost, and what you can do yourself and what you cannot.

"I'll do it myself to save some money!" said many of our students, prior to paying more to have it fixed later.

When it comes to renovations, please do not try and do everything yourself. Know your limitations. I know that I can paint, and when I was starting out, I would do the painting. It was actually kind of therapeutic in a way. I could see something from start to completion; in my line of work, there is a lot of in-between time. Painting a house over the course of a weekend was very satisfying to me, and even though I am not a professional painter, for me to save thousands of dollars when I was starting out, it made a lot of sense. Now, if you asked me to do the plumbing, or renovate the kitchen or fix a screen door, I was not your guy. I am admittedly one of the least handy guys going, and for that reason, I would happily contract out the work to other people to ensure that it got done correctly.

Who should never do the work? The tenant. When I first started out and did not know too many handy people, and was trying to save as much money as possible, I had at times allowed the tenant to do the work themselves. I will never forget my tenant, James. Good old James, the handyman who never finished anything! I had a pretty shabby duplex as one of my rental properties, and James offered to redo the kitchen if I bought the materials. I thought to myself that it was a great idea, and it would save me money, build up my equity, and James, my tenant, would be happy too. He went out and bought the materials, gave me receipts, and I paid him for what he purchased. To this day, I am quite sure all the materials did not make their way to the house. James lived in the unit for about 18 months, and his idea to renovate the kitchen started in month 2. By the time he moved out, the kitchen still had no counter top. Half the kitchen cupboards had no doors, there was no backsplash, and it needed paint. By the time he moved out, I actually had to redo the whole kitchen over again! When you have a tenant do the work, you have limited to no recourse on what they are going to do, or when they are going to get the work done, because the perception is that the tenant is giving YOU a deal, not the other way around. When you hire an independent contractor, you pay for a portion of the bill upfront, and then you do not pay the balance until the work is completed. Typically, someone who is renting, if they offer to do renovations for you, they are not going to cover your materials upfront either.

Having a tenant do renovations also leaves payment up in the air. Do they get a reduction in rent? If so, you are reducing your income, but you are missing out on the expense as well. In order to keep your records clean, do not ever reduce the rent. Keep it the same and consistent, and if you do find yourself in this type of situation, keep all other side transactions separate from the rent.

When it comes to renovations, do what you say you are going to do. This will be a no-brainer for some of you, but for those of you whose favourite words are, "No problem; I'll get to that right away," and then tomorrow never seems to come, you need to up your accountability game. If you have any major issues, and they do not get addressed, your tenant will be able to drag you to the Landlord and Tenant Board, and you will be found in the wrong. It is imperative that when you find out about major issues, such as water leaks, heat problems, bed bugs, etc., you take immediate action. The problem may not be solved right away, but you must be able to demonstrate that you contacted a qualified professional to help you take care of the situation in a reasonable amount of time. If a tenant calls and advises that the heat is out, in January when it is -20 degrees, and you don't call anyone for 3 days because it was Friday and you were on a holiday, and you did not get back until Tuesday, this is not acceptable! Get a list of qualified professionals that you can trust for major issues. Heating and air conditioning, plumbing, roofing, electrical, and a general handyman should all be on your contact list.

Full-on property management is definitely an option but should be worked into your cash flow numbers upfront. If you are purchasing your property out of town and know that you will be completely hands- off for the management, be sure to account for all of the maintenance costs of the property in your monthly cash flow. I took on a property manager for my units when I got to the 15-unit mark. As I truly love to teach, and get more joy out of that than managing properties, it was a business decision to outsource it to another company. This was a great learning opportunity for me. Property managers will not only charge you for the management of the tenants but also for the management of the tradespeople when they are doing renovations. For example, when you hire a plumber, you will be billed for them calling the plumber, meeting the plumber at the location, and even for paying the plumber. With my first property manager, I did not look at all my receipts for some time, and it turned out that I was being billed 3 and sometimes 4 times to "pay" the same tradesperson. Because the tradesperson was doing different jobs at the same property, there were multiple invoices for paying the same person, which I thought was excessive. Having a property manager give you a predetermined markup for each job is a great way to manage expectations. That way, you know exactly how they are getting paid; and that way, it controls the costs and keeps them accountable. In this type of setup, the property manager would send you the actual receipt or invoice for the work competed, in addition to the markup. For example, if there was a plumbing repair for $500, and the markup is 10%, then you know exactly how much they are being paid for their work.

Serve Your Paperwork on Time, ALL THE TIME

There are no awards for the world's nicest landlord. I have fallen into this trap more times than I like to admit, where a tenant has said to me that they could not pay the rent because of an accident, job loss, sick dog, or dying relative. The reality is that you can still say, "I am so sorry to hear that, but I have to give you the eviction notice." Many times, a tenant will say that they will have you all paid up in a week, or 3 days, or 2 weeks. Whatever it is that they say, you can always reply with, "No worries, but I still have to give you the paperwork; however, it does not mean anything if you pay all the money in full when you say you are going to." This way, you are keeping them accountable to when they say they are going to pay. The biggest mistake I have made with all my rentals in the past is waiting to file for eviction notices. If you are really on your game, it can still take 6 weeks. However, if you delay 2–3 weeks, or even a month before starting, you could be out 2 months of payments before anything happens. Don't let this happen to you; do not become emotional with the relationship. It is a business, and if rent is not paid on the exact date it is due, then it is nothing personal. The bank is never going to wait for your mortgage payment, so why should you?

Rental Increases

We teach all of our students to give rental increases on the anniversary of the move-in. The Landlord and Tenant Board will announce each year what the allowed rent increase is, and it has

Long-Term Management of Your Rental

typically been anywhere from 1–2% in the past 10 years. This may not seem like a lot; however, it will seem like a ton when you go to sell the property one day, and your rental unit is severely under market rent because you did not keep up with increases. By keeping up with the increases, it is not only good for your pocket book but will make your property more marketable when you go to sell it in the future. If you have a tenant paying market rent, then you may have another investor purchase your house; whereas if you have a under market rent property, the only person that is likely to purchase your house is one that wants to use it as an owner occupied. The reason being is that you cannot evict a tenant just because the rent is too low. Our costs are going up every year—from hydro to property taxes to house insurance—so ensure that you keep your rental increases consistent as well. There is no Oscar or Grammy Award for the country's nicest landlord.

So, you have done all the work, and you have a property that has a ton of equity in it—what do you do with it? In the next chapter, we are going to discuss exactly how to utilize the equity you have built up in your rental property, in the most profitable, stress-free, and tax-efficient way.

Chapter 9

The Sale or Refinance of Your Rental

"A goal without a plan is only a dream."
– Brian Tracy

Now, this step may seem like a long time away; however, if you have been doing the work and making plans up until this point, it will be here before you know it! I hit my mission of being mortgage free after being in home ownership for just over 10 years. When I had purchased my duplex, it was just under 4 years later that I moved out of that house and moved into another house. I kept it as a rental property and moved into something else. I was fortunate to have some amazing tenants, and literally just cashed cheques on that property for years after I moved out. I was concentrating on building my business, my mortgage brokerage, my family, and eventually purchasing my dream home. The beautiful thing about rental properties is that your capacity to handle more, grows with the more properties you get. Your life will continue to grow, and you will be surprised by how what seems so daunting right now, will become second nature to you in a couple of years.

After 10 years, you will come to a crossroad, and some of you well before this. You will reach a time when you need to decide what to do with your rental—do you sell it, or do you refinance it and keep playing the game of Monopoly? I made a decision to sell my very first rental after owning it for just over 10 years, when I was 34 years old, as I had always had the mission and the dream of being mortgage free by the age of 35. I want to be clear that SELLING the rental was not necessarily the best thing for me financially—but emotionally, it was. I wanted, and needed, to achieve my dream. By achieving a dream and goal so big after so long, it gave me a deep sense of pride, accomplishment, confidence, and power. This, to me, was worth more than any amount of money. There will come a point in your life, as it does with all of our students, where you will be thinking more about what you want your life to look like, instead of just your bank account. By selling the rental property and being mortgage free, it gave me tremendous freedom, and that is why I decided to sell the house instead of refinance it. We are going to go through both options here now, and as you will see, both of them can be quite similar depending on your situation. There are a tremendous number of variables that can change the outcome, but our goal for all of our students is to arm them with the ability to choose. What was best for me may not be best for you, but by having the knowledge, you will be armed with the financial tools to finish your own personal plan, whatever it may be.

Selling Your Rental Property

When you are approaching the 10-year mark for holding your rental, you want to start to pay attention to the market conditions that are in that area. Your local real estate partners will be able to advise on whether or not things are up or down. You want to start to plan the sale of your house, where you can make that huge prepayment on your home. In conjunction with

The Sale or Refinance of Your Rental

this, you want to ensure that you have planned your mortgage maturities to run simultaneously with the sale of the house. If you have a needless penalty, it can eat up some serious dollars of your equity at this point. When you are approaching the end of your 5-year term, and you see that prices may have dipped a bit in the past couple of years, then ensure that you renew your mortgage into either a 1-year term, open term, or another variable rate term. Again, the variable rate options will carry the least penalty. Let's not forget that if you have tenants paying off your property, another year of keeping it will only mean more money in your pocket at the end of the day. At this time, you will likely be very close to having the equity built up in your rental being sufficient to pay off the balance on your primary residence. By selling the home, you will incur a capital gains tax on the sale. This is a form of tax that is calculated on the difference between the sale price, less expenses like major renovations, and the purchase price. After 10 years of appreciation, this can likely add up to quite a bit of money. You want to ensure that you plan for it, as it is a nasty expense to come up unexpectedly. Capital gains are currently taxed on 50% of the profit, at your marginal tax rate. Your marginal tax rate is based on all of your income together for that tax year. If you have a big capital gain and are working with other sources of income, you will likely be pushed into the highest tax bracket for that year, which could be anywhere from 40–50% of your income. Let me give you an example. I have a client, Dave, who purchased a rental property 6 years ago, in an up and coming area of Hamilton, for $200,000. He rented it out and made some renovations over the years, and he ended up selling it for $650,000. His capital gains tax was based on the following:

Sale Price – $650,000
   Less R/E Costs – $32,500
   Less Legal Costs – $1500
   Less Renovations – $20,000
   Less Purchase Price – $200,000
   Less Purchase Price Costs – $4000
Total Profit Over 7 Years = $392,000
Approximate Capital Gains Tax = $88,200
Net Profit After Taxes = $303,800

In Dave's example, he had a huge tax burden; however, he was able to pay off the balance of his mortgage! He was able to get rid of all of his bad debt in order to be mortgage free. Now, this does not mean he was taking all of his cards off the casino table; he was now able to re-leverage and purchase more real estate with his house. That's right; he took out another mortgage on his house, for approximately $400,000, which was the down payment for 2 more rentals. Now all of the debt that he had was GOOD debt! It was tax deductible! It was important for him and his family to live mortgage free. This was a personal goal, and it allowed him to pursue a different career that he was passionate about, and the financial flexibility to go after his new dream.

Refinance or Remortgage Your Rental Property

Another option for you at this time is to refinance your rental property. What this means, specifically, is increasing the mortgage on your property, based on the new appreciated value. The benefit in this scenario is that you are taking the money out of your house, tax free, in that you do not have to pay the capital gains tax on the portion of funds that you have refinanced, or remortgaged in this case. Under current mortgage rules, in Canada, you are only able to refinance up to 80% of the value of your house. This means that you are not getting access to approximately 20% of the equity that you would have got if you were to sell it. Typically, when you are refinancing any house, the value is based upon a market appraisal. An appraisal will take into account recent properties that are similar to yours, and what they have sold for in the past 6 months, in order to get a reasonably accurate number for the value of your property. The unfortunate part with an appraisal is that you will more than likely end up with a value that is at least 5% below the actual market value of what you would sell it for. In the above example, this would be like valuing the house after real estate costs are paid. In addition, appraisals are based on the past, not where the market is going. In addition to that, they do not take into consideration private sales, or properties that have not actually closed. This means that if someone has sold a property, but the buyer has not actually taken possession yet, the property could be right next door to yours but would not be used as a comparable. All of these factors lead you to getting LESS money out of your rental property in order to pay off the mortgage on your house where you live.

Let's use the same example as we did above to compare, and assume that my student, Dave, refinanced his property instead of selling it.

Sale

Sale Price – $650,000
    Less R/E Costs – $32,500
    Less Legal Costs – $1500
    Less Renovations – $20,000

Less Purchase Price – $200,000
Less Purchase Price Costs – $4000
Total Profit Over 7 Years = $392,000
Capital Gains = $88,200
Net Profit After Taxes = $303,800
PLUS, Equity Build Up = $70,000
Total Mortgage Prepayment = $373,800

Refinance

Appraised Value, 5% Below Market Value – $617,500
New Mortgage for 80% of the Above – $494,000
　Less Existing Mortgage – $130,000
　Less Renovations – $20,000
Proceeds to Use for Principal Mortgage Pay Off = $364,000

　As you can see in Dave's example, there was not a HUGE difference in the 2. He came out about $10,000 ahead with the sale of the property, and in his case, he wanted to purchase rental properties in different areas. He thought the one that he had, capped out, and he was very excited to pay off his mortgage in full. He would have been short with the funds from the refinance; therefore, the sale was the right decision for him.

　In the refinance option, you are not saving the capital gains tax; you are just deferring it, as it will still be payable at some point in the future, just not at this time. That is the major benefit to doing the refinance option. The drawback comes with the extra money that is being taken out in order to pay down your principal residence. As this money is not being used for additional investment, it is technically not tax deductible. In the example above, by adding $364,000 to the rental property mortgage, this is money that is not being used to generate income, and therefore it is not tax deductible. You would only be able to claim the interest on the original amount. I have had many students that will take the risk with the tax man, and continue to write off the interest on the mortgage, but like we said, the pig can get fat, but the hog will get slaughtered. If you are ever going to take this risk, know what your future potential liability could be in the case of an audit. In this case, if Dave had done the refinance, and continued to use all the interest on the mortgage as a tax deduction, he would be writing off approximately $4000 of interest each year. This would equate to him having LESS taxable income. If, after 5 years, he was at a tax bracket of 40%, this could add up to $1600 of extra taxes each year for 5 years, or a total of $8000. I do not endorse this strategy, knowing full well it happens quite often.

Lastly, when it comes to refinancing the property, you need to be sure that you will still cash flow the property. What that means is that you want to ensure that as your mortgage is being raised quite substantially, as such, the mortgage payment will go up as well. You do not want to do the refinance at the cost of having a loss every month, where the rental income is not enough to cover the expenses. This was another reason that Dave decided to sell his property in the example above. The rents had not kept pace in order for the increased mortgage payment to be covered by the existing rental income coming into the house.

FREE BONUS: If you are in this situation right now, email our team at **freeme@getmortgagefreefast.com**, and we can do a no-cost comparison for you. Just put "Sell or Refi?" in the subject line, and one of our "getmortgagefreefast" agents will be in touch.

Many of our students, after doing this and teaching this for over 10 years, decide to keep the rental properties and refinance the mortgage. The reason they do this is that their plan actually changes, to amass much more property, and they start thinking of building a legacy for their family instead of just paying down the mortgage. We also go into great detail in our coaching program about doing a hybrid option. What happens in some cases is that you do not need to take out all the equity available from your rental property when it comes time to remortgage, as you may only need a portion of it in order to pay off the balance of your existing mortgage. In these options, we take out as much equity/money as possible while still ensuring that the property maintains a positive cash flow—ensuring that the rents are still exceeding all the expenses, including the new, higher mortgage payment.

When it comes time to choose, make sure you do the work. Get in touch with one of our coaches to help you weigh out the options. A mortgage broker can run both scenarios for you, and the only cost to you will be the cost of an appraisal, under $500, in addition to your time, not to mention that $500 is a tax deduction. If your numbers come back positive based on the appreciated value of the house, and you have enough to pay off your primary, and you are still in a positive cash flow situation, then go for it! If, on the other hand, you had a goal similar to mine and want to see it through to the end, by all means sell it. I guarantee, as it does with all our students, both scenarios feel pretty damn good at the end of the day! The good news is that by sticking to your plan, after 10 years, you will have multiple options, and all will be financially freeing!

Now, speaking of sticking to the plan, give yourself a pat on the back for getting this far already! That is also what the next chapter is all about. The plan is long, but the destination is huge. You will need some tools to help you stick to your plan. In the next chapter, you will see how you can keep true to your plan

The Sale or Refinance of Your Rental

and set up systems to win, and become mortgage free, really fucking fast!

Chapter 10

Stick to Your Plan

"Whether you think you can, or you think you can't, you are right."
– Henry Ford

Well, here you are at the last chapter; you know how to do it! You are unstoppable, you are excited, and you are ready to take on the world and pay off your mortgage really fast! That is, until tomorrow, when you go to work and one of your co-workers say, "Hey, I just found the deal of the century; we should invest in THIS!" Tomorrow or the next day, or the day after that, is when all hell is going to break loose on your plan that you just finished making and getting excited about. The reason is that as human beings, we are always looking for the EASY way out—a quicker, better way to do things and get things done!

To this day, I still look for easier ways to do things. As I write this—financially secure with millions in equity from sticking to my plan of buying and holding properties—I just went through the numbers of a joint venture I did with someone as a buy, hold, and flip, and I only made 4.5% on my money. What a bunch of shit! The reason I share this is that even for me, it is difficult to practice what I preach. Even I need constant reminders of what works and what does not, and unfortunately, those reminders can be a lousy return, like 4% on your money. Or even worse, it could be a condo project that you purchased, put money down as a deposit, waited 3 years, went through a massive growth spurt in the economy, and the condo development went broke—and they were never built! This happened to me too. Yes, I got my money back, but what did I lose? I lost massive buying power. If I would have taken that $50,000 and purchased a single family home, and rented it out to someone, not only would I have seen over 25% in growth (this was the Hamilton market from the end of 2015 to the beginning of 2018), but I would have also had over 3 years of the principal being paid down; not to mention any cash flow on a month to month basis that would have accumulated.

I tell you this to STICK TO THE FUCKING PLAN! I am yelling this at you now, as every time that I deviated from the original plan, I never came out as good as when I stuck to the original plan. Over the last 15 years, I lost out on 2 condos, spent 18 months buying, renovating, and selling homes with a full-time contracting crew, tried joint ventures that were quick in and outs, and nothing worked as well as buying and holding rental properties for the long term.

Since you have finished this book, you are likely a pretty savvy person already, and someone that sees things through. Unfortunately, the stats are that only 15% of people that actually purchased this book will finish it, so good for you! However, being a savvy person, you are likely to have multiple streams of knowledge coming at you by listening to lots of podcasts, and you are probably part of a least one investment club as well. I believe these are all good things to be a part of, but this is your moment to listen, and listen well. I have taught this to hundreds of people and have seen the rewards they have gotten; it works for the people that make it work. Following the 10 simple steps

Stick to Your Plan

above will get you mortgage free really fast. The best people in the world have coaches, from Tiger Woods to Kawhi Leonard of the Toronto Raptors 2019 NBA champions. If you do not have a coach, you do not have someone to keep you accountable. Doing what is right is easy when you are excited, and I would say that by getting this far, you see the light for yourself, as you are excited!

Accountability is required when excitement wears off, and that is what a coach is there to do for you. I encourage you to commit and enroll in our "getmortgagefreefast" coaching program, and do the work! If you have made a decision, email us at **freeme@getmortgagefreefast.com**, and put "Sign Me Up" in the subject line, and we will fast track you for the first 12 months. How many shoes do you think Nike would have sold if the slogan was, "Just think about it?" Take massive action now, in order to be committed to your plan. Take an action that will keep you accountable. If you are like many people, myself included, where you read a book like this and don't do any of the work along the way, do yourself a favour now, and email info@getmortgagefreefast.com, saying, "I want to be mortgage free!" This will keep you accountable and get the process started for you to achieve your goal.

Change is hard in the beginning, messy in the middle, and beautiful in the end. When people try to lose weight, they will typically fail before they start. You will decide that you are going to lose 10 lbs, and then something comes up—the wedding, the cottage get away, the girl's weekend. There is always a reason NOT to even start. Before you know it, a year has gone by, and you have actually put on 5 lbs and not taken off the 10 you originally wanted to. The toughest part is starting. Now, imagine that you start that diet, and you actually get 2 weeks into it; you will start to notice a difference. Your pants feel a bit looser, and you get a couple of extra compliments, and that becomes your fuel! That propels you to keep eating healthy and losing weight. That is where you actually get some momentum. The same will happen once you start the 10 steps to getting mortgage free fast, and stick to the plan. You will start to show yourself who is boss, and you will be setting and breaking new barriers on your own limitations that you have had for years. After some time, you will hit another lull in productivity. You may see the first 5–10 lbs go pretty quick, but then it might be another month before you start to shed any more weight. During this time, it is easy to become discouraged and start to look for another way for things to get done. This is where the rubber hits the road, as they say; this is where your true test of character is built. This is where you are building up the foundation of your mental skyscraper. By continuing to have your discipline, and sticking to your plan, your foundation of confidence will become rock solid.

Have you ever seen a construction company working in the ground on a huge tower before? They are typically in the ground for 12–18 months; not to mention the years of planning that goes into it before they even break ground. What most people see is floor after floor going up every week, where it looks like 20 floors of a building went up in a couple of months. This is how your family and friends will see you after 5 years of sticking to your plan. They will see the confidence you have, your financial savviness, and then, one day, they will see you sell your investment property for hundreds of thousands of dollars, in order to pay off your mortgage. Taking action will always lead you to the next step you have to make. Taking action creates accountability. Taking massive action will create massive results. Taking little action will result in little results! Take massive action now, get a coach from "getmortgagefreefast," and change your life.

If you want to fast forward your plan, take out more equity as it is growing, and purchase more properties. I have had students do this in as little as 4 years, with a lot of discipline and the right road map. With the right guidance and the correct purchases, you can have money working for you while you are working at your job. This truly creates an unparalleled compound effect for your money to grow. The more leverage you have in real estate, the more your appreciation is growing, and the more principal you are paying down each month. Do not try another plan in order to speed things up; look at how you can enhance your existing plan. Stay on the destination, but by all means, whether it is with this program or another one, hire a coach to keep you accountable. This can only be done if you start with purchasing the first investment property. Without the first one, you will never be able to fast forward to another one and another one. If you are like many of our students, you have already said to yourself at some point, "I wish I would have bought something last year, or 2 years ago, or 5 years ago." None of our students have ever said that again. Make sure you don't turn that into a song on repeat that you sing to yourself every year for the next 10 years.

I want to leave you with how being mortgage free has truly changed my life. I actually work harder today than I did 15 years ago, but it is for a much different purpose. I told you earlier that I just recently purchased my first exotic car, the Mercedes AMG GT. I love it so much that it was worth mentioning twice. For the car lovers out there, it is totally worth it! I am enjoying every minute of the life I chose. I did not sacrifice anything when I really look back on it. At the age of 40, I am driving with the top down to look at cottages (that I can actually afford now), spending time with my daughter, and thinking to myself that this is awesome! This is what it is all for. The journey was worth every second of pain that it took. The mental state that being mortgage free puts you in is not a fleeting achievement. It is one that you can continually rest on, appreciate, and operate from.

To the little voices that are saying, "Here is the sales pitch," listen up and listen good. The reason I wrote this book, and continue to work so hard, is because someone wrote a book that changed my life, and lots of people along the way took the time out of their busy lives to help improve mine. I feel it necessary to pay it forward to other people. Lastly, is it wrong to love what you do? Is it really working so hard if you are enjoying all that you do? If you cannot answer NO to these questions yet, then you have not had the time to really think about what you want to do. I would love to give you the gift of time, in order to find those answers.

A word of caution for you, from my own experience: You will be tempted to deviate from this plan if you choose to take it. I often encourage people to take risks and educated chances on business, and the grass will often seem greener, easier, and quicker other ways, but remember the following story. When I paid off my house, I followed my dream and launched Mission35 Mortgages in honour of my dad. I was already operating a mortgage franchise for another company, and when I pitched the idea to my team, I was met with something I did not anticipate at all. The majority of my team left. I had spent over 5 years growing, teaching, and educating my team on how to build a business—pouring my blood, sweat, and tears into them—and thinking that they would love the idea and help grow the new vision I was creating. When we officially opened the doors, I was down from a team of almost 20 people to a skeleton staff of 5 people. I instantly lost almost $250,000 of revenue overnight, from making the decision to follow my dream.

I had purchased a larger building to accommodate my

anticipated growth, and spent hundreds of thousands of dollars on the renovations; not to mention that in the same year, my mother passed, and my daughter was born. It was by far one of the most stressful years of my life, in hindsight. In one decision, I had lost thousands of dollars, and a team that I thought of as close friends, and I had a huge uphill battle in front of me just to get back to where I was. I am proud to say that after 3 years of hard work, it is now one of the top mortgage brokerages in Canada, the highest google reviewed, and employs some of the best people in the industry. I tell you this because, going through all that turmoil, with going to one hospital and seeing my mother pass, and then going to another hospital to visit my wife because of some pregnancy complications, I don't know if I would have been able to do it if I was still worried about making my mortgage payment. I may have said FUCK IT, and just gone back to work for someone else, and given up on my dream. Being able to chase your dreams from a place of mortgage free, and of financial security, will empower you to deal with the inevitable shit that is going to come your way. When you are financially secure, you can deal with the lows better, and have a much better perspective and positive outlook on what the future will hold for you. The journey is worth it. The sacrifices are worth it. The tears are worth it. You may have already encountered things like this on your journey, and if you have not, I am sorry to say, but they are coming. My mission is to help you to prepare for them the best way I know how, and that is to get your finances in order fast.

  As I sit in my boardroom of one of the commercial buildings I own, I am at peace with whatever happens. Whether my books sell or not, and whether my seminars are full or empty, I can still continue to do what I love, which is educating people on their finances and how to not only make more money, but to keep more of the money that they make. The reality is that I have made more money in the years since I became mortgage free, than in the 10 years prior to me being mortgage free. I have done it with more fun, ease, and passion than I ever thought imaginable. I used to listen and read like a sponge on how to make money, and one of the top things I heard people say was that if you find your passion, you will never work a day in your life! I used to think to myself, whenever I heard that, "What a bunch of bull shit! How can I find my passion when I am trying to pay my mortgage and put food on the table?"

It was not until I became financially secure that I truly was able to let my passion find me. It took the security of knowing that I would be okay, and that my family would be okay, no matter what event hit us, to open up to the idea of having a passion. A passion will pull you into work; it will wake you at night, and it will bring you into the office on a sunny Saturday afternoon to finish a book. The passion will bring you limitless income as well. This is why you need to stick to the plan. You may hate rental properties, and you may hate investing in real estate, but you do want to become mortgage free; and I can tell you firsthand that it is the worthiest financial goal to pursue, as quickly as you can. When you have become mortgage free, another life opens up, with possibilities you never imagined. Take the ride; it's a long one, and you will want to quit and get off at many points, but just like any trip to a worthy vacation destination, you have to go through the long line ups to get to the beautiful beach.

BONUS CHAPTER

I DON'T QUALIFY!

*"Don't take no for an answer,
until you give someone the opportunity to say yes!"*
— some smart guy somewhere

"I don't qualify," is something I hear a lot today. You may have gone to a bank, and the bank said, "No way, buddy!" You may have inquired with a mortgage broker, who did not even call you back. Well, you did not call *my* company, obviously (shameless plug). The harsh reality is that in the mortgage market of the future, the banks are going to say no to almost half of the population in Canada, and that number will likely increase. With new financial rules and regulations coming in that are tightening up lending policies for banks, it is time to get creative with how you can get money in order to purchase your next house. For some of you, you may have skipped right to this chapter because you have already tried, or you currently own a house, and something has happened along the way, where you feel like you can't get any more funding. Well, there is hope—not all mortgage lenders were created equal, and there is never a shortage of money.

In order to get my first rental property, I had to make a business case to borrow money from my dad. I purchased my first house, which was a duplex, and I rented out the nicer 3-bedroom unit, and was living in the much smaller, uglier, 1-bedroom unit. In order to pay the bills, I had to have the other unit rented out, or else I would not have been able to pay my bills. I was making a salary then of approximately $30,000 per year, and I felt pretty good about myself as soon as I moved in. I was like, "DAMN, I can have friends over, girls over—I have made it." It wasn't until I was having my first BBQ on my back deck that I realized, "Wow, if I do everything right, I will be in my 50s when this thing is paid off." That is when I had to start thinking outside the box, and brainstorming as to how I could get my next property. I barely had enough money to pay the bills, let alone get a down payment for another property. I would have to save for another 5–10 years in order to get enough money. That is when I approached my dad to lend me the money for a down payment on another property.

My dad was a very conservative investor; his vehicle of choice was Guaranteed Investment Certificates and Canada Savings Bonds, both of which would pay approximately 2–3% interest rates in a year—not exactly like winning the lottery. I found a property with 3 rental units in it (a triplex), and showed my dad the revenue from rents—less the mortgage payment, taxes, insurance, and paying his loan—and how much money I would have left over. I offered him a rate of return of 6% on his money, which was more than double what he was getting on his usual investments, and I showed him how I planned to have him paid back in 2 years. Now, I am quite sure he was a little sceptical about the whole thing, but being my dad and my biggest supporter, he went for the investment; not to mention that he gave me the absolute third degree on everything I presented to him. To this day, I would say he was by far my toughest sale. After purchasing that rental property, I was actually able to pay him back in just over 1 year, which was much quicker than what he anticipated. I want to show you how to make this happen—where there is a will, there is way—you just have to be willing to look outside the box. In this chapter, we are going to talk about higher interest loans, joint venture partnerships, as well as the Boomer Bank!

High Interest Loans and Private Lending

This is a segment of the mortgage market that has increased exponentially since the government introduced the "stress test." That is where borrowers have to qualify at a significantly higher rate than the one they will actually be paying; not to mention there was a major rule change called the "B20" guidelines, which major lenders and banks have to abide by, and which severely limits the amount of income you can use to qualify someone who is self-employed. Go figure; we are in the midst of the largest increase of self-employed people in history, and our government makes it harder and more expensive for them to borrow money. That is for another book. The good news is that there is hope.

Private loans or private mortgages do not have to abide by the same rules and regulations as conventional banks do. As a private lender, they are allowed to lend out their own money any way they wish to, under their own rules and guidelines. Now, as you can imagine, they are doing so at a much higher rate than a bank. This is an option for you to look at for your next approval. If you have a plan in place for a rental property, and you have a down payment, this may be a viable option. However, you must have a hard look at your cash flow on the rental property, as your cost of borrowing will be significantly higher, and you want to make sure it does not push you into a negative cash flow position. A private loan can act as a bridge for you, meaning that a good mortgage broker will help you make a plan for what you need to do in order to get the next loan at a better rate. I have seen many clients get an investment property, where they were paying interest-only payments at a rate of almost 3 times the going bank rate. However, the reason they did it was that they had a mild setback, such as a job change, where they could not meet the income requirements for another year, or a credit setback where we were able to coach them to get their credit back on track within 12 months. As long as you can cover the monthly expenses, and have a CLEAR exit strategy on how you are going to get out of the higher interest loan, this is an excellent way to start getting into the real estate market today, rather than waiting for things to get better.

Don't Obsess Over the Rate

I have had many students say, "I am going to wait, because I can only qualify with a private lender or a trust company." This is very short-sighted. Let's say you were to purchase a home today in an up and coming market for $450,000. Let's also say the mortgage you were getting is $360,000, and the rate you have to pay is 6%, when the banks are giving away money at under 3%. The difference of interest in 1 year on $360,000 is $10,800. Let's imagine that you are purchasing in a reasonably appreciating real estate market, which would be at a rate of 3%. An increase of 3%, on a home that is $450,000, is $13,500. This means that the house would be worth $463,500 when your credit is better. In addition, if you choose a mortgage that is amortized, meaning that you are paying off principal AND interest, you would pay off approximately $7000 in principal as well. This means that by paying a higher rate of interest, and not waiting until the stars align and everything is perfect, you are still ahead by over $10,000!

Joint Ventures

Gone are the times when we have to be the solo riders and do everything all on our own. If you are not in a space to purchase your first rental property, or even your first house for that matter, get some partners. If you have a good plan in place, with sound financials, you will be able to find other people to invest with you. You may only have $20,000 of available equity or down payment to purchase a home, and may need $80,000 in order to make it work. All you need is 4 other people, just like you, in order to get your $80,000 together. Now, your pay off at the end will not be the same as it would be if you did it on your own; however, I would rather have 25% of something than 100% of nothing. I have purchased several properties with partners, and it is a great way of getting into something that you normally would not have.

I purchased my first apartment building with a partner, who is also a close friend of mine. The initial investment was approximately $150,000, and it was much easier for me to come up with $75,000 at the time, than it was to come up with the entire $150,000. Not only that, but it was easier to get the borrowing we were looking for, as there were 2 of us for the bank to have as security instead of just one. The power of leverage works whether you are doing it all on your own or with partners. A great place to find partners is by associating with the right people. If you are at the pub every night, well, you might have a hard time. However, a couple of great places to start would be joining either the REIN network (Real Estate Investment Network) or the REITE club (Real Estate Investing

Training and Education). The REITE club has meetings on a monthly basis, and at each meeting, you can identify what you are looking for, whether it be properties to invest in, partners to invest with you, or money to invest in a project you have. You are who you associate with, so if you are thinking that you can't find anyone to invest with, well then, grow your network, dude! The only thing limiting you is you!

Free Bonus: If you feel like you have tried everything, and still think you have no hope, email our team at freeme@getmortgagefreefast.com, and we will do a no-cost, 30-minute consultation on your situation to see what can be done. In the subject line, put, "There is still hope."

The Boomer Bank

You are in the most amazing time of your life right now, in order to have your parents, family, or friends, who are baby boomers, invest with you. Equity has risen for people who have been home owners for the past 10 years, by hundreds of thousands of dollars, and they are used to getting marginal returns and paying high management expense ratios on their existing mutual fund and stock portfolios. Many of the people in this demographic are looking for alternative investments such as real estate, but they lack the knowledge or trust to have someone show them the way. Why not be the one who shows them the way? You could approach someone like this, who has equity in their home, and show them that it is possible for them to qualify for the mortgage, and to get a secured line of credit on their home, with a bank, at a low interest rate, and you can be partners! The bank can be anyone—stop limiting your thinking. Your bank can be anyone who has money or equity and wants to invest with you. I have had many students that find family members to invest with them, where they are what is referred to as the "working partner." The working partner is responsible for all the tenant management, paperwork, upkeep, and basically any problems that arise. There is tremendous value to this position in a relationship.

As I said before, if you don't have the money, than you have to have time. Make the time to put the plan together, and show someone how much money they can make over the next 5–10 years by purchasing a rental property with you. The other partner in this scenario is called "the money partner"—surprise, surprise! Noah, one of my most recent students, who is only 19 years old, pitched an opportunity to his parents to co-invest in a rental property. His parents took a line of credit on their house for the down payment, and co-signed with him for the mortgage. He is now the proud owner of a rental property, at 19 years old. If you think your parents will say no, re-read the quote above: *"Don't take no for an answer, until you give someone the opportunity to say yes."* As a dad myself, there is nothing that I would want more than for my daughter to be financially secure.

Parents would love to invest in their children. Not only does it bring you closer together and give you a common bond, but who better to make money with than with family! If you are going to pitch to family, they will likely be your worst critic; but remember, they love you and want to help you. Make sure you know your shit before you present to them. Don't make up the numbers, and ensure that you have a solid plan in place, with ALL of the questions ready to be answered that they will surely ask. Do not—and I repeat, DO NOT—bullshit them. If you do not know the answer to something, then tell them, "Good question," and find out the answer. This will build your credibility with them. Finding a Boomer Bank is much like finding your dream partner. You might have to ask a lot of people before they actually say yes. It's like when babies are learning to walk: They don't just try once, fall on their face, and say, "Fuck it, I guess I wasn't meant to walk in life." They get up, and they fall; they get up and fall again—and they get up again and again until they walk. You need to have the same commitment to finding a money partner as you did learning to walk. If you have that type of tenacity, you will surely find at least one, if not have your pick of who, to invest with.

With any type of partnerships that you are going to create, whether it be with a family member, joint venture partner, or just a money partner, remember that you do not have to give everything away, NOR do you need to keep everything for yourself. As you can see from my example of investing with my dad, I was able to pay him a high interest rate on just the down payment. Had he asked me for 50% ownership of the whole property in order to invest with me, I would have likely said yes to that. However, it is good to start with what you are looking for, and still leave room for concessions. In the case that you do not get what you are asking for, you can settle for less, as long as it is creating a win- win for both of you. If you have a very heavily one-sided arrangement with a partner, I assure you that resentment will build from the other side. The last thing you want is a partner that is not happy with how things are going. All successful partnerships are formed at the beginning by dealing with any possible problems or exits.

Jamie, one of my students, purchased his first rental property with friends. They did not have an agreement in place; they just simply split everything but put the mortgage in his name. This was fine until later, when he wanted to continue to build his portfolio, and it was negatively affecting his approval limits but not affecting his "silent partners" at all. Luckily, he was able to approach them to sell the property, and they agreed to it. Had it not gone smoothly, it could have hurt not only his future investment plans but also his long-time friendships. Take the time to set up exit strategies upfront. If you think the divorce rate is high today, the partnership break-up rate will blow your socks off. This is meant not as a deterrent but as a tactic. I am in several real estate ventures today, which are all win- win and have clearly defined exit strategies. For example, I have one with a partner where we both agree to refinance the properties we own, every 5 years, to take out as much money as we can. At that time, we either choose to re-invest our money together again or we don't. If one chooses not to, then we don't re-invest the money. It is unemotional because it is a rule; and when you take emotion out of the equation, you can keep friendships intact.

Now, if you have read the above, and your little voice is still saying, "I tried all that, and it doesn't work," then you need to take a different course, one that is about not being a negative little bitch. The above will work—it will just take more work! I want things to be easy, just like you do. Unfortunately, the greatest things that I have accomplished in my life have never worked out to be that way. There is no reason for you not to pay off your mortgage fast now, but it is up to you to take the next step—the only question is, will you?

About the Author

Brian Hogben became mortgage free at the age of 35 years old. His goal, which was inspired by his dad ever since he was a child, was to be financially secure on his 35th birthday. Brian sold the first investment property he had ever bought, in his 34th year, in order to pay off the balance of the million-dollar home he currently lives in today. Unfortunately, his dad was not there to see his goal turn into a reality. He died 2 years prior, from leukemia. The passing of Brian's dad, and the accomplishment of such a huge milestone, inspired Brian to open a company that could inspire and instill the same values that his father did. Mission35 Mortgage was created out of this vein. Mission35 is a company that is committed to helping people increase their wealth through the ownership of real estate.

Brian wrote this book in order to show other people that becoming mortgage free, many years earlier than what typical Canadians think is possible, is not just a pipe dream but a reality—a reality that gave Brian a life of purpose and a huge amount of courage once the goal was achieved. The 10 steps in this book, if followed correctly, can give ANYONE the ability to have confidence in their finances and their entire financial future. The options that open up to you once you have financial security, meaning your bills are paid every month with certainty, are endless. You can leave a job you hate, or a boss that you despise, and open up the business, or follow the path of the career you always dreamed of. This is possible when you are mortgage free. When you have a huge asset and your living conditions paid for and accounted for, it is MUCH easier to take a leap of faith and pursue what you truly want.

The motivation for this book was Peter Hogben. Brian's dad was a pillar in the family. Even though he never made more than $60,000 a year in his life, he was able to raise a family with 2 boys, pay off his mortgage, and retire comfortably, all before the age of 60. Peter was a very happy and content man, never spending more than what he made. He did not have a lavish lifestyle; however, he never wanted for anything, and he always had the time to do exactly what he wanted, which was to spend time with his family and take his kids to all of their sporting events. This was the motivation for Brian, not only in growing up but also in writing this book, in order to show people that the fruits of a financially healthy lifestyle can lead to more joy, especially when reducing the wants.

By following the 10 steps that he writes about in his book, Brian has accomplished more being mortgage free than he ever did on the journey leading up to it. His company, Mission35 Mortgages, in just 2 short years, was nominated as one of the best new brokerages in Canada. It was the top google reviewed mortgage company in Canada, with a 4.9 rating, and continues to break sales records each year. Brian is able to follow in his father's footsteps by being able to attend all of his daughter's dance routines and soccer practices. Being mortgage free has allowed the freedom to choose a lifestyle that allows him to put family first, and still push the limits of his growth from the comfort of knowing that if the big plans don't work out, his family will still be taken care of. This sense of purpose has propelled Brian into giving more of his time to teach people about financial security and financial literacy, in order to give them the chance to have the same opportunities that he did.

About the Book

This book will answer the question of whether you spent too much on your house or not. Quickly, you will understand that becoming mortgage free does not mean never spending any money at all, or never having any fun. It means ensuring that you have the right house, and *more importantly*, the right mortgage on your house. *How to Get Mortgage Free Fast* will give you the confidence to go house shopping for not just one house but for two. Through getting the right mortgage on your house, and spending the appropriate amount of money, you will be able to get approved for a 2nd mortgage. This book will not push you to become a professional landlord, but it will show you how and why you need to purchase a 2nd house. The equity you build in a 2nd property will build exponentially faster than it would through any type of mutual fund, stock, or other investment tool. Purchasing another property gives you massive leverage in order to grow your wealth. No matter what age you are at, there is no wrong time to start. If you are 25 years old, the strategies can be done, using your parents. If you are in your 50s, and are wondering if you will ever become mortgage free, this book will give you the tactics and steps to follow.

Five Things This Book Will Show You

1. The right house and mortgage for you
2. How you should set up your mortgage in order to get mortgage free (It's not what you think!)

3. The difference between good debt and bad debt (You actually will need more debt in order to get out of it!)
4. How you should purchase a rental property (You will buy one rental property and hold it for 10 years in order to make the biggest mortgage prepayment of your life.)
5. How to get massive tax advantages through owning real estate and creating a fun, part-time side hustle (It's not about how much money you make; it's about how much you keep at the end of the day.)

After reading this book, you will have a specific strategy and time frame in order to become mortgage free. Each step will give you more and more confidence in seeing that becoming mortgage free is an actual possibility for you. *How to Get Mortgage Free* actually paints the target on the wall for you to shoot for. The journey to becoming mortgage free is as exciting as the destination—who you become, and the financial savvy you will get along the way, will propel you to higher and greater wealth than you ever thought possible. This is the best gift you could give to yourself and your family. As you will see in *How to Get Mortgage Free Fast*, the journey truly starts once you become financially secure, as everything becomes a possibility.